3D SCROLL SAW
PROJECTS

35 Fun Compound-Cut Designs, More Than 150 Designs

From the authors of

SCROLL SAW
woodworking
& CRAFTS

FOX CHAPEL
PUBLISHING

© 2025 by Fox Chapel Publishing Company, Inc.

3D Scroll Saw Projects is an original work, first published in 2024 by Fox Chapel Publishing Company, Inc. The patterns contained herein are copyrighted by the author. Readers may make copies of these patterns for personal use. The patterns themselves, however, are not to be duplicated for resale or distribution under any circumstances. Any such copying is a violation of copyright law.

ISBN: 978-1-4971-0488-4

The Cataloging-in-Publication Data is on file with the Library of Congress.

Managing Editor: Gretchen Bacon

Acquisitions Editor: Kaylee J. Schofield

Editor: Joseph Borden

Designer: Mike Deppen

Proofreader: Kelly Umenhofer

Indexer: Jay Kreider

To learn more about the other great books from Fox Chapel Publishing, or to find a retailer near you, call toll-free 800-457-9112, send mail to 903 Square Street, Mount Joy, PA 17552, or visit us at *www.FoxChapelPublishing.com*.

We are always looking for talented authors. To submit an idea, please send a brief inquiry to acquisitions@foxchapelpublishing.com.

Printed in China
First printing

Contents

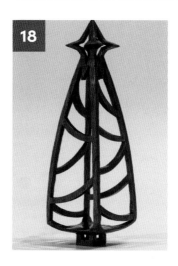

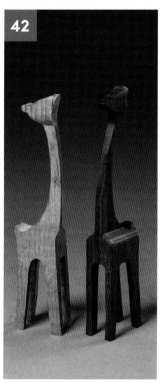

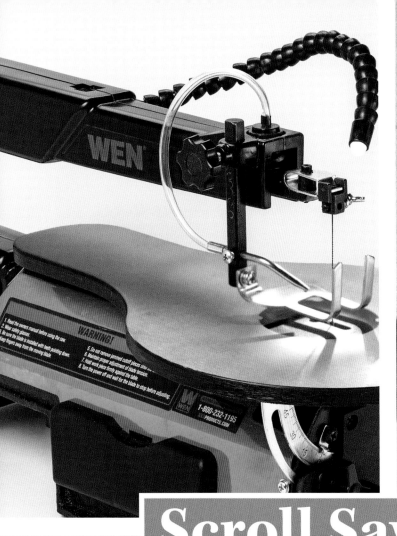

Scroll Saw Basics

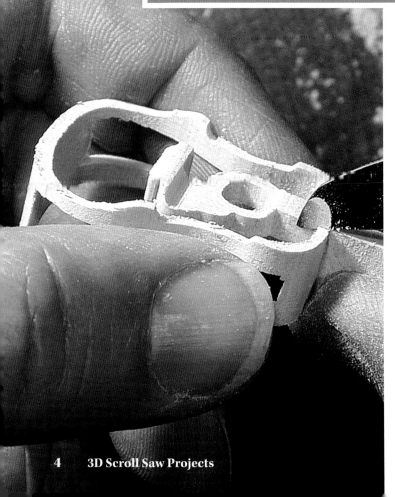

What Is a Scroll Saw?

A scroll saw is an electrically powered saw with a reciprocating blade that moves up and down to cut through wood and other materials. One of the main advantages of a scroll saw is its removable blade, which you can easily insert into a predrilled hole and cut outward from the center of your project. Thanks to the scroll saw's versatility and ability to handle curves, tight corners, and tricky cuts, it is an excellent choice for creating beginner-friendly projects. Since the blade and saw are fixed, your job is to move the workpiece around, rather than moving the tool in relation to the workpiece. You're in control! Remember to go slow, have fun, and let the blade do the work.

Materials and Tools

Only a few tools are needed to complete the projects in this book, and they're probably already lying around your shop. You'll need a scroll saw and blades, of course, your choice of wood, sanders for preparing and smoothing blanks, and a drill press and bits.

Other Useful Items

- ❏ **Masking tape, blue painter's tape, clear packaging tape, temporary-bond spray adhesive, and glue sticks:** For attaching patterns to wood.
- ❏ **Finish:** Danish oil or mineral oil are common food-safe finishes but use your finish of choice.
- ❏ **Mineral spirits or commercial adhesive removers:** To aid in removing paper patterns from wood.
- ❏ **Sandpaper:** For smoothing pieces of wood before and after scrolling. You'll want to have a variety of grits up to at least 400 grit.

Sanding through the Grits

The grit number on a length of sandpaper refers to the average number of particles per square inch. The lower numbers, such as 60 and 80, are the coarser grits, which remove the most wood and are used for rough shaping. The higher numbers—220 and above—refer to finer grits that remove less wood and are used for smoothing. "Sanding through the grits" simply means using progressively finer sandpapers to smooth the scratches left by coarser grits. Rub sandpaper on a project until the wood is smooth and shaped the way you want. Then move on to a finer grit of paper and repeat, sanding with the grain when possible.

Safety

Take the time to properly prepare your workspace so that your scrolling experience is safe and enjoyable. Work in a well-ventilated space and surround your setup with good, even lighting. Always wear a dust mask and safety goggles, tie up long hair, and secure loose clothing before beginning a project in your shop. When using power tools, such as drum sanders and band saws, employ a benchtop dust collector to help keep your work area clean and protect your lungs (see Sidebar below) to ensure that you can scroll without difficulty for years to come.

Wear protective gear, such as masks and safety glasses, to protect your eyes and lungs from wood dust.

Why is Wood Dust a Health Concern?

Wood dust is considered carcinogenic to humans. Exposure to certain kinds of wood dust has been associated with health issues due to the natural chemicals in the wood, or substances in the wood such as bacteria, mold, and fungi. Wood dust is also associated with irritation of the eyes, nose, and throat; dermatitis; and respiratory system effects including decreased lung capacity and allergic reactions. It is imperative to wear personal protective equipment while working with wood. Always research a wood's toxicity before beginning any project.

Choosing Wood

The projects are presented with wood and drill bit dimensions, as well as a recommendation on which wood to use. Here, we've listed some common wood varieties you may find useful. If you'd like to try some fancier woods, mahogany, purpleheart, and zebrawood, are popular choices. Whenever using a new or rare species, be sure to learn about its properties, as many exotic woods have harmful toxins.

Basswood: This light, soft wood is consistent in grain and takes paint well, making it a great starter wood for beginners. Woodworkers based in Europe will find limewood to be a suitable substitute.

Cherry: This hardwood has a rich, reddish hue and is similar to walnut in hardness. Cherry burns easily when cut with a power saw, so make sure to cover the wood with clear packaging tape before applying the pattern. In addition, you could use a large skip-tooth blade, as this can reduce the amount of dust that gets caught in the kerf (the cut path created by a blade).

Maple: Dense and light in color with a distinctive grain, maple is highly prized by woodworkers. Just make sure to apply clear packaging tape to the surface of the wood before attaching a pattern, as maple can burn easily.

Pine: Light-colored and beloved for its affordability and ubiquity, pine is a great starter wood for beginners to scrolling. However, it can be porous in places, increasing the chance of breakage on delicate projects.

Poplar: Soft and easy to work with, poplar often takes on a slight greenish tinge once a finish is applied.

Walnut: This durable wood is prized for its workability and deep, chocolatey color.

Selecting a Blade

Not only do blades come in different sizes, but the cutting teeth come in different configurations and different numbers of teeth per inch (TPI). As a general rule, the thickness of a blade increases as the numbers ascend; for instance, a #3 blade will have a smaller kerf (the width of the cut left by the blade) than a #7 blade and will be better suited for detail work, or thinner pieces of wood. You'll use two main blade types for your people and pet projects:

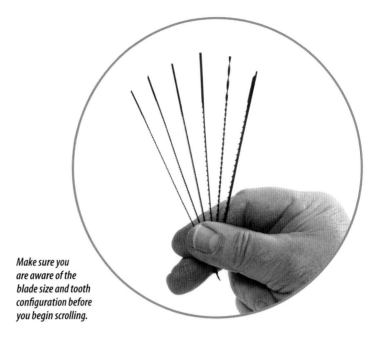

Make sure you are aware of the blade size and tooth configuration before you begin scrolling.

Skip-Tooth

Skip-tooth blades are the most common configuration. Instead of having one tooth right next to the last, they skip one tooth, leaving an open space between the teeth. The space helps clear sawdust and allows the blade to cut faster. Skip-tooth blades produce a slightly rougher cut surface, so you will likely need to sand after cutting.

Skip-tooth blade.

Reverse-tooth blade.

Reverse-Tooth

Reverse-tooth blades usually follow the skip-tooth or double-tooth configuration, but with the bottom couple of teeth pointed in the opposite direction from the rest. These teeth cut as the saw blade travels upward. Where skip-tooth and double-tooth blades splinter the bottom of the blank slightly, reverse-tooth blades remove these splinters. Reverse-tooth blades produce a cleaner bottom cut than other blades, but they don't clear as much sawdust. The sawdust can slow the cutting and possibly heat the blade, making it more likely to break or scorch the wood.

Matching Wood to Blades

WOOD	THICKNESS	BLADE SIZE
Hardwood, softwood, plywood	¼" (6mm) or thinner	#2/0 to #1
Hardwood, softwood, plywood	¼" (6mm) to ½" (1.3cm)	#1 to #2
Hardwood, softwood, plywood	½" (1.3cm) to ¾" (1.9cm)	#3 to #4
Hardwood (less dense), softwood, plywood	¾" (1.9cm) to 1" (2.5cm)	#4 to #6
Hardwood (dense)	¾" (1.9cm) to 1" (2.5cm)	#5 to #7

Choosing a Finish

You can finish the projects in this book in a number of ways. A food-safe finish is recommended, especially if the projects will be handled by young children. Most finishes are food-safe when fully cured; however, always read the manufacturer's instructions thoroughly before applying a finish to any project. *Note: Be sure to dispose of oil-soaked rags according to the instructions on the package of finish, as they can spontaneously combust.*

Acrylic Paints, Stains, and Dyes

If you do not want to leave your projects natural, you could apply color to your project with transparent stains or washes of water-based acrylics. The benefit of a transparent stain or paint wash is that it allows the attractive woodgrain to remain visible. You could also choose to use glossy paints because they eliminate a finishing step by acting as their own topcoat.

Finish your projects with paints, stains, or dyes, if desired.

Food-Safe Finishes

Carnauba wax: Derived from the Brazilian palm tree, this wax is harder and more water-resistant than beeswax. Used as a light protective coating or topcoat polish, carnauba wax is a popular choice for woodworkers.

Danish oil: Highly versatile, water-resistant, and food-safe when fully cured, natural Danish oil is a popular choice for toys. It dries to a hard, satin finish and will darken the wood slightly. It can be combined with oil-based pigments to create wood stains.

Mixture of mineral oil and beeswax: Easily whipped up and applied, this mixture ensures the longevity of your projects. The simple mixture not only restores and protects but also leaves your items with a light scent of honey.

Raw linseed oil: Not to be confused with boiled linseed oil (which can contain toxic additives), this simple, flaxseed-derived oil is hard-wearing, water-resistant, and suitable for use on hard or close-grained wood.

Shellac: Harvested from a bug in India, shellac is a versatile, nontoxic wood finish that enhances the natural grain while adding smoothness without the plastic-like qualities of polyurethane or lacquer.

Tung oil: Extracted from nuts, tung oil often requires numerous coats. It leaves a natural finish that darkens the wood while showcasing the grain. Once thoroughly cured, it is food-safe.

Clear Finishes

Clear spray or brush-on finishes provide a final sealing coat that boosts resistance to chipping and moisture without obscuring the woodgrain. Acrylic, lacquer, or polyurethane sprays typically come in several varieties, ranging from matte to gloss.

Whether you leave your project natural or decide to add a colored finish, spray the finished piece with a clear finish to prevent chipping and damaging the woodgrain.

Ornaments

Musical Instruments

Develop your compound-cutting skills with delicate designs

BY STEPHEN MIKLOS

These ornaments are beautifully intricate, elegant, and nearly as fragile as glass ornaments, so when I give or sell them, I provide a sturdy gift box filled with wood excelsior (wood shavings used for packing). They always make for great conversation pieces and welcome holiday gifts. I first became aware of the potential of delicate compound-cut scroll sawing when I saw geometric ornaments at a farmer's market. Since I make musical instruments, the first thing I thought to apply this technique to was an ornament in the form of a mountain dulcimer. Later, I made a guitar ornament.

MATERIALS

For the Guitar
- ❑ Wood blank: ¾" (19mm) thick x 1³/₈" x 4" to 5" (3.5 x 10.2 to 12.7cm)

For the Dulcimer
- ❑ Wood blank: ⁵/₈" (1.6cm) thick x 1³/₈" x 4" to 5" (3.5 x 10.2 to 12.7cm)

- ❑ Emery boards
- ❑ Spray lacquer or finish of choice
- ❑ Aniline dye (optional)

TOOLS
- ❑ Drill press with bit: ⅛" (3mm) diameter
- ❑ Scroll saw with blades: #5 crown-tooth, #5 skip-tooth
- ❑ Carving knife
- ❑ Chisel (optional)

COUNTERING CURLY CHIPS

Inevitably, when trimming your ornaments, you will get small fringes or curly chips. I attack these with emery boards that I have cut into narrow strips on my scroll saw.

PATTERN LOCATED ON PAGE 102

Getting Started

Before you begin, cut the wood to the proper dimensions, and make sure the edges are square and true. Fold the pattern along the line shown, and attach it with the fold running along the edge. Then, use a ⅛" (3mm)-dia. bit and drill where indicated on the pattern. Be careful to drill straight through, especially when drilling into the sides. A drill press will make this much easier.

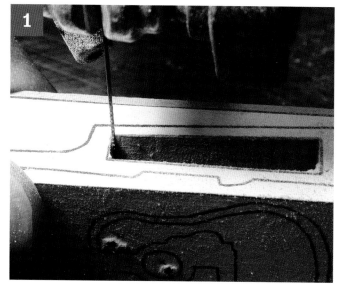

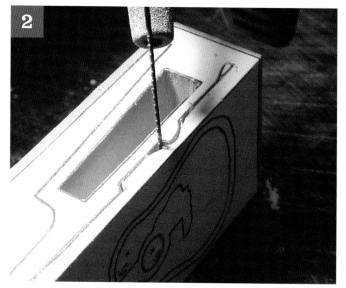

1. Cut out the inner part of the guitar body. All the inside of this cut is waste, so feel free to cut a curve at each corner, cleaning the corners up after removing the waste piece. If the resulting block doesn't slide out easily from both the top and bottom of the hole, then check the squareness of the table to the blade before continuing. All the cuts from the side should be done with minimum pressure and maximum patience.

2. Cut along the upper face of the guitar. Use the waste on the upper side to make your sharp corners where the fret board ends and at the front of the bridge.

3. Cut the underside of the guitar. This cut doesn't connect to the previous cut. The cuts from the face side will release the top and bottom ends of the guitar from the block.

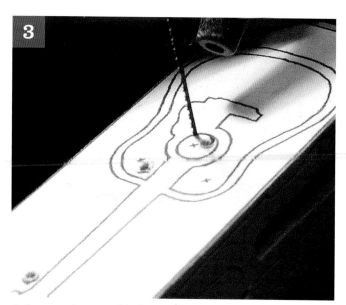

4. Cut out the sound hole. Lay the block flat, thread the blade through the hole in the middle of the sound hole, and cut out this circle.

5. Cut around the outside of the sound hole, pick guard, and bridge. Continue around the inner outline of the body. This cut will release three rather interesting pieces of waste.

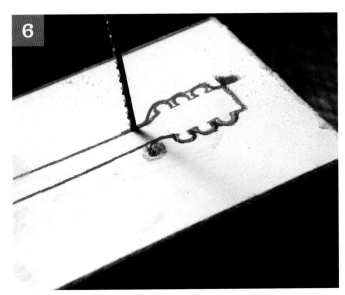

6. Cut around the outline of the guitar. Use the waste around the peg head and shoulder to cut from different directions to define the corner and the curves around the tuning buttons, or you can use on-the-spot turns to accomplish the same thing.

7. Carefully remove the pieces from the blank. After the outline has been cut around, the guitar and several waste pieces should come right out of the blank. Making the last cut one continuous sweep around the outline assures that the piece comes smoothly out of the block, even if there was a slight error in squareness of the blade.

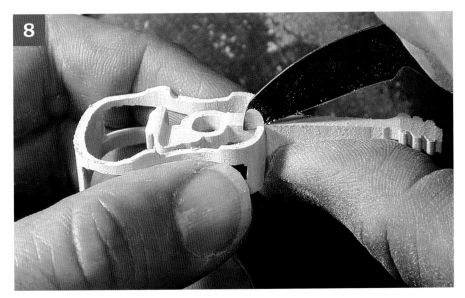

8. Trim the sides. Cutting the contour of the bridge and the fret board leaves humps on the face of the sides that need to be whittled away with a sharp knife. Make a stop cut along the edge of the fret board before trimming the sides in this area. While doing any knife trimming, be sure to hold the guitar by its neck or base; the sides are extremely fragile due to short grain.

9. Finish trimming the ornament. Trim the tuning buttons down to make them stand back from the face of the peg head. Then trim off the copy of the sound hole, fret board, and pick guard inside the outline of the back of the guitar. I trim this off with a knife or chisel.

10. Finish your ornament, using your method of choice. I find that spraying a clear finish like shellac or lacquer is easiest. I use glossy spray lacquer. If you use a light-colored wood like pine or poplar, you can dye the wood by dipping it in an aniline dye before spraying. I find the ornament is too delicate and complex to use any rubbed or brushed finishes.

Feathers and Leaves

Indulge your inner free spirit with these whimsical compound-cut creations

BY SUE MEY

CUT BY STAFF OF *SCROLL SAW WOODWORKING & CRAFTS*

These leaf and feather designs are inspired by childhood memories of exploration through forests unknown and traipsing home with pockets full of these treasures. These compound-cut ornaments require a bit of concentration to make, but the payoff is huge. Attractive hardwoods, like oak or cherry, lend themselves to the feather and leaf designs, but you could also cut them from a bland wood and finish with stain or acrylic paint. Remember, when cutting the side-view pattern, you will be cutting wood that is about 2" (5.1cm) thick, so choose your wood accordingly.

MATERIALS

- ❏ Cherry, lacewood, or oak wood blanks: ¾" (19mm) thick x 2" x 5 ½" (5.1 x 14cm)
- ❏ Spray adhesive
- ❏ Sandpaper
- ❏ Clear packaging tape
- ❏ Finish, such as semi-gloss spray lacquer or Danish oil

TOOLS

- ❏ Scroll saw with blades: #3, #7 skip-tooth
- ❏ Drill press with bits: assorted small
- ❏ Vacuum

Instructions

1. **Photocopy the pattern and fold on the dotted line.** Apply spray adhesive to the back of the pattern, align the fold with the corner of the blank, and press it into place. Drill holes for each fret.

2. **Make the cuts on one face.** Use a #3 skip-tooth blade. I start with the frets on the front of the feather or leaf and work outward. Then, cut the perimeter. Remove the dust with a vacuum, and tape the cut pieces back in place.

3. **Rotate the blank 90 degrees.** Then, cut the remaining face. Use a #7 skip-tooth blade. Remove the feather or leaf from the blank, and carefully sand away any blemishes or bumps. Finish with semi-gloss spray lacquer or Danish oil.

PATTERN
LOCATED
ON PAGES
103–104

Snowflake Ornaments

Combine fretwork snowflakes with wooden bulbs to make elegant ornaments

BY SUE MEY

CUT BY LELDON MAXCY

Compound-cut ornaments are easy to make. In fact, you can complete one with just a few cuts. The snowflake accents are easy to cut. You can also fill the recessed space with a photo or initials to personalize the ornament.

MATERIALS

- ❏ Wood blanks: 2" (5.1cm) square x assorted lengths (see the patterns)
- ❏ Wood blanks: ¼" (6mm) thick x at least 1¼" (3.2cm) square
- ❏ Spray adhesive or glue stick
- ❏ Cyanoacrylate (CA) glue
- ❏ Clear tape
- ❏ Sandpaper
- ❏ Clear spray finish

TOOLS

- ❏ Scroll saw with blades: #9 skip-tooth
- ❏ Drill press with bits: assorted small, Forstner 1¼" (32mm) diameter

Making the Ornaments

1. Cut the wood to size. Fold a pattern along the dotted line, apply adhesive to the back, align the fold with the corner of a blank, and press the pattern into place.

2. Drill the hanging hole (if marked). Drill the blade entry holes for the inside cuts, and cut the inside frets on both sides.

3. Cut the perimeter on one side, making a single continuous cut around the ornament. Secure the cutoff pieces with clear tape, and cut the other profile. Remove the waste, and sand away any rough spots.

Adding the Inlay

4. Stack together several pieces of ¼" (6mm) thick wood. I suggest using a color that contrasts with the ornaments. Drill blade-entry holes and cut the snowflake inlays.

5. Separate the stacks and sand the snowflakes smooth. Use a 1¼" (32mm) diameter Forstner bit to drill a ⅜" (1cm) deep hole in each bulb ornament for the inlay.

6. Smooth the edge of the drilled hole, and glue the inlay in place using cyanoacrylate (CA) glue. Apply a clear spray finish.

PATTERN
LOCATED
ON PAGES
105–106

Snowflake Ornaments **17**

3D Christmas Tree Ornament

Test your precision on a wicked wire-thin project that pulls no punches

BY CLAYTON MEYERS

This thin design requires precision and accuracy to achieve a uniform look. I finished this hardwood version with a high-gloss polyurethane for a long-lasting protection that will reflect the lights on my Christmas tree, but you can modify the wood choice and finishing method as desired.

MATERIALS

- ❑ Wood blank: 1½" (3.8cm) square x 5¼" (13.3cm) long
- ❑ Spray adhesive
- ❑ Sandpaper, assorted grits
- ❑ Clear packaging tape
- ❑ Clear spray finish, such as high-gloss polyurethane
- ❑ Ribbon or hook (for hanging)

TOOLS

- ❑ Scroll saw with blades: #5 skip-tooth
- ❑ Drill press with bit: ⅛" (3mm) diameter
- ❑ Jeweler's files
- ❑ Combination square

Getting Started

1. Choose a variety of hardwood with a tight grain structure. I used cherry for this piece but find that maple and walnut work nicely as well.

2. Attach the pattern views to two adjacent sides of the blank using spray adhesive. Use a combination square to verify that the wood blank is perfectly square at all four corners. Drill the blade-entry holes for all interior cuts on both sides of the blank.

3. Lightly sand the pattern-free sides of the blank. You want it to sit flush on your cutting surface. Ensure that your scroll saw blade is perfectly plumb before you start cutting, as any fluctuation of the blade will cause the wire frame of the tree to look thinner on one side than the other. It could also lead to a very weak structure on the finished product.

Fine-Tune Your Force

In compound-cutting projects, the thickness of the wood you cut through changes dramatically as you move through the project. Be sure to constantly adjust the amount of force used to avoid over-cutting.

Cutting and Finishing

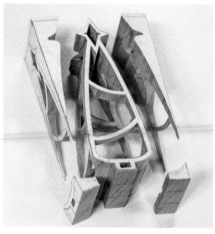

4. Make all the interior cuts on one side of the blank. Then, rotate the blank 90 degrees, and make all the interior cuts on the second side. Using the same type of blade, begin the outside cuts. Make all outside cuts in one pass and save the scrap pieces. Stay as close to the pattern line as possible, cut slowly, and use a sharp blade. You should now have four pieces of exterior scrap removed from the first side.

5. Tape the scrap pieces back onto the piece exactly as they were before. Rotate the ornament 90 degrees, and make the outside cuts on the final side. Remove all of the scrap to reveal the Christmas tree. Sand and finish the final piece to your liking. Add a ribbon or hook to display it on your tree.

Change Blades Often

Cut slowly and change blades often. When you're cutting through thick hardwoods on a scroll saw, the first sign of a dull blade is that the wood begins to burn. You may not notice this right away, so pay close attention to the area you're cutting in order to avoid harming the project with skewed cuts.

Finial Ornaments

Fun compound-cut designs can be made from solid or laminated wood

BY SUE MEY

Compound-cut ornaments can be made from a solid piece of wood and painted or stained, or finished naturally. To give the ornaments a unique look, glue up your blank using thin strips of contrasting wood. I cut my stock slightly oversized and sand it down to 1¾" (4.5cm) square. For straight blade-entry holes and neat inside cuts, the blocks must have perfectly straight edges at a 90-degree angle to each other. If you are not laminating your blank for a multi-colored ornament, you can skip right to step 3.

MATERIALS
- ❏ Wood blanks 1¾" (4.5cm) thick:
    - ❏ For large ornaments: 1¾" x 5⁵⁄₁₆" (4.5 x 13.5cm)
    - ❏ For medium ornaments 1¾" x 4⅛" (4.5 x 10.5cm)
    - ❏ For small ornaments 1¾" x 3" (4.5 x 7.6cm)
- ❏ Masking tape
- ❏ Clear packaging tape
- ❏ Wood glue, for laminating strips of hardwood
- ❏ Sandpaper, assorted grits up to 320
- ❏ Deep-penetrating furniture wax liquid or Danish oil
- ❏ Lint-free cloth
- ❏ Clear spray varnish

TOOLS
- ❏ Scroll saw with blades: #9 and #12 skip-tooth (or blades of choice)
- ❏ Drill press with bit: ⅛" (3mm) diameter
- ❏ Disc sander
- ❏ Needle files
- ❏ Stiff-bristled paintbrush
- ❏ Medium-sized artist's paintbrush
- ❏ Clamps
- ❏ Table saw (optional)
- ❏ Scraper (optional)

PATTERN LOCATED ON PAGES 108–111

Finial Ornaments **21**

Glue Up the Blank

1. **Cut the strips to size.** I cut an assortment of ¼" to ⅜" (6mm to 10mm) thick wood into 1⅞" (48mm) wide strips. Cut the strips into 5½" (140mm) long pieces. Shorter pieces can be used for smaller ornaments.

2. **Glue the strips together.** Mix and match the strips of wood for unique color combinations. The stack should be about 2" (51mm) thick. Apply wood glue between the layers, and clamp the strips together until the glue dries.

3. **Sand or trim the blank down to 1¾" (45mm) by 1¾" (45mm).** I use a disc sander, but you can use a table saw or your method of choice. It is critical for the sides to be flat and square to each other. Cut to height as desired for the size of ornament you intend to make.

4. **Cover the blank with masking tape.** Fold the pattern on the dotted line, and attach the pattern to the blank. Drill the blade-entry holes with a ⅛" (3mm) diameter bit. Remove the rough edges with sandpaper or a scraper.

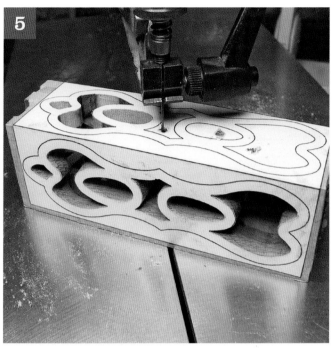

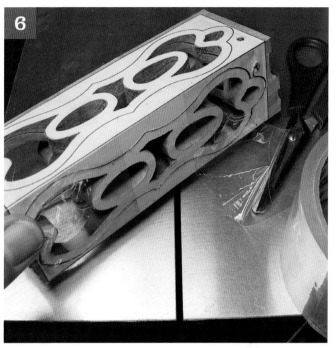

5. To cut the fretwork, I use a #9 blade for soft woods and a #12 blade for the laminated blanks. Cut the frets on one side, remove the waste, and then turn the blank and cut the frets on the adjoining side.

6. To cut the perimeter, start with the end-grain area. Cut the entire perimeter on one side. Then, hold the ornament and waste in place while you wrap clear tape around the blank. Rotate the blank and cut the perimeter of the ornament on the second side.

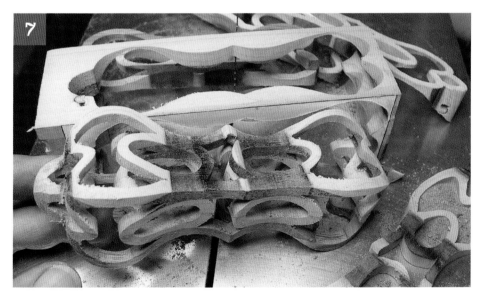

7. Remove the waste wood and sand the ornament with 320-grit sandpaper or needle files. Remove the sanding dust with a stiff-bristled paintbrush, and apply a deep-penetrating furniture wax or Danish oil. Allow the finish to dry, and remove any excess with a dry lint-free cloth. Then apply several thin coats of clear varnish.

Present Ornament

Scroll the shape and peel off the waste to reveal a gift that keeps on giving

BY CLAYTON MEYERS

Although it may look complicated, this compound-cut project is simple to make. The majority of the design makes use of the squareness of the blank and relies on interior cuts to give it a three-dimensional look. This reduces the amount of scrap that needs to be reattached, as would normally be the case with other compound projects. I chose hard maple for this project, but any tight-grained wood, such as walnut, cherry, or birch, would also work well. Finish the piece with a high-gloss spray to reflect the lights hanging from your tree.

MATERIALS

- ❏ Wood blank: 1½" (3.8cm) square x 5¼" (13.3cm) long
- ❏ Spray adhesive
- ❏ Sandpaper, assorted grits
- ❏ Clear packaging tape
- ❏ Clear spray finish, such as high-gloss polyurethane
- ❏ Ribbon or hook (for hanging)

TOOLS

- ❏ Scroll saw with blades: #3 skip-tooth
- ❏ Drill press with bit: ⅛" (3mm) diameter
- ❏ Combination square

Getting Started

1. Choose a type of wood. Attach the pattern views to two adjacent sides of the blank using spray adhesive. Use a combination square to verify that the wood blank is perfectly square at all four corners. Drill the blade-entry holes for all interior cuts on both sides of the blank.

2. Lightly sand the pattern-free sides of the blank so that it will sit flush on your cutting surface. Ensure that your scroll saw blade is perfectly plumb before you start cutting, as any fluctuation of the blade will cause the present to look thinner on one side than the other.

PATTERN LOCATED ON PAGE 107

Cutting and Finishing

3. Make all the interior cuts on one side of the blank. Then, rotate the blank 90 degrees, and make all the interior cuts on the second side. Stay as close to the pattern lines as possible, cut slowly, and use a fresh blade. Note: While you are making the cuts after rotating 90 degrees, the thickness of the wood will vary depending on what portion of the piece you are cutting through. Avoid exerting too much force, as you can easily overcut the line while traveling into a thinner portion of the blank.

4. After finishing the interior cuts, begin on the outside cuts. Make all outside cuts for the first side in one pass, saving the waste pieces for later.

5. Using clear packaging tape, tape the waste pieces to the block exactly as they were before. Rotate the ornament 90 degrees, make the outside cuts on the final side, and then remove all of the waste wood. Sand and finish the piece to your liking; I used assorted grits of sandpaper and a high-gloss polyurethane. Apply several coats for a durable, long-lasting finish. Add a ribbon or hook to display it on your holiday tree.

Shimmering Icicle Ornaments

These "frozen" compound cuts are the perfect addition to your wintry décor

BY AL BAGGETTA

No two icicles are exactly alike; wind, temperature, and water determine their final shapes. For these icicles, you cut the blank from two viewpoints, and when you are finished, a 3D icicle will emerge from the scraps. Add some paint and glitter to transform your wooden icicle into a fashionable ornament. If you are worried about straying off the cutting line, you're in luck: this project will still produce many beautiful ornaments even if you veer a little off course. In fact, you might end up with an even more unique icicle.

MATERIALS

- ❏ Wood blank: 1" (2.5cm) square x 8" (20.3cm) long
- ❏ Masking tape or blue painter's tape
- ❏ Spray adhesive or glue stick
- ❏ Sandpaper, assorted grits
- ❏ Spray paint, such as flat white
- ❏ Glitter, such as silver or white
- ❏ Finish, such as clear spray (optional)

TOOLS

- ❏ Scroll saw with blades: #5 reverse-tooth
- ❏ Drill press with bit: 1/16" (2mm) diameter
- ❏ Sanding wheel or mop with 150-grit sandpaper (optional)

Getting Started

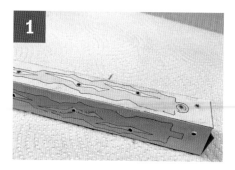

1. Prepare the wood. Cover the two adjacent faces to which the pattern will be attached with masking or blue painter's tape. Attach the pattern using spray adhesive or a glue stick. Then drill the blade-entry holes.

Cutting

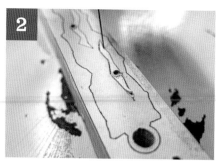

2. Make all of the interior cuts on one side of the blank. Rotate the blank 90 degrees. Make all the interior cuts on the second side, and then cut the second side's perimeter. Tape the waste pieces back onto the block exactly as they were before. Make the outside cuts on the first side, and then remove the waste wood.

Sanding and Finishing

3. Refine the icicle's shape with a sanding wheel or mop. For any fuzzies left behind in the interior cuts, carefully run a folded piece of sandpaper along the edges of the cuts. For a frosty look, spray-paint the icicle with flat white paint. While the paint is still wet, sprinkle with silver or white glitter and let dry. If you used a hardwood, you could just finish with a clear spray for a natural look.

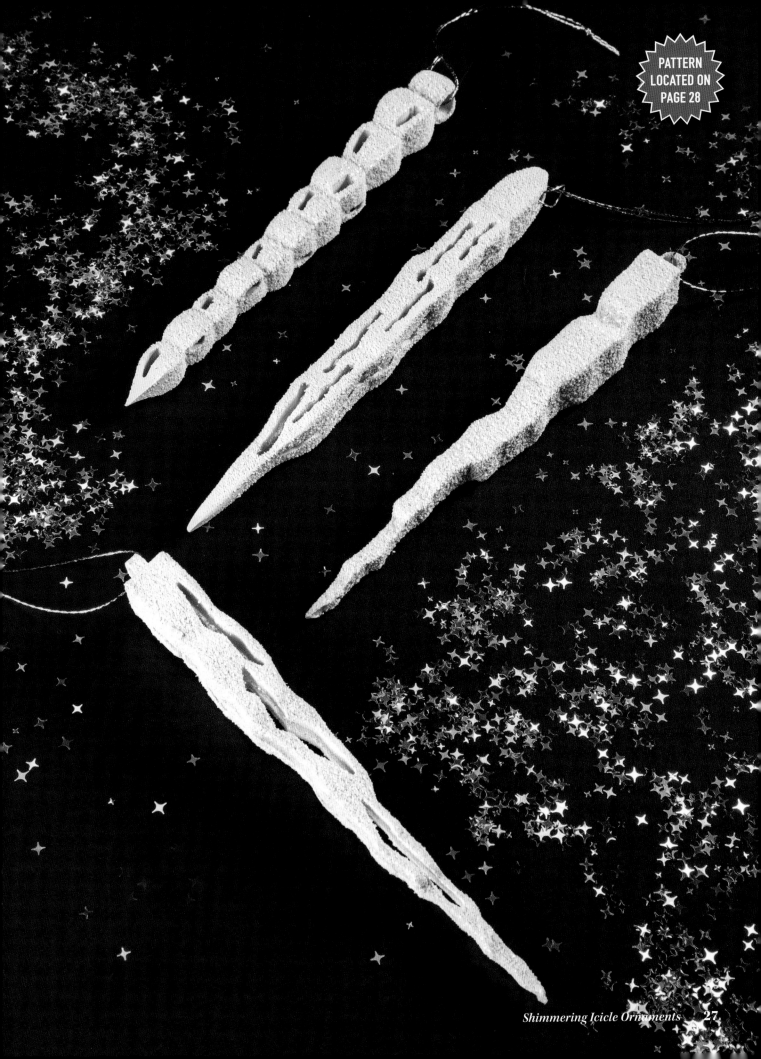

PATTERN LOCATED ON PAGE 28

Shimmering Icicle Ornaments **27**

Shimmering Icicle Ornaments

Photocopy at 100%

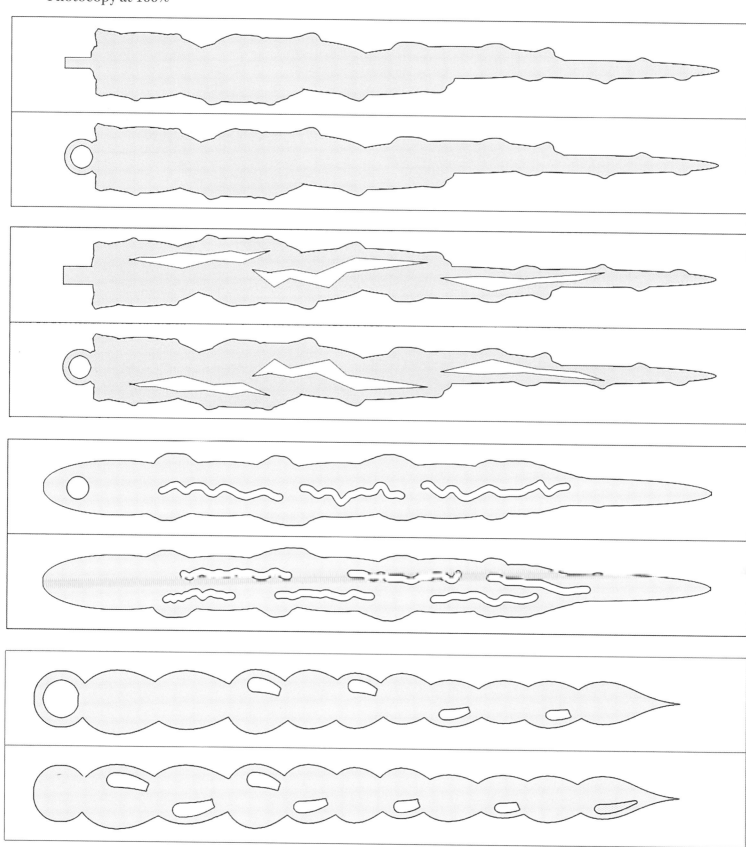

Gifts

Ornament Earrings

Don these decorative baubles and look as snazzy as the Christmas tree

BY DENNIS KNAPPEN

DESIGN BY SUE MEY

These designs are simple to cut, but you can execute them in dozens of different ways, so each one you create will have a personal touch. Layer your hardwood scraps to make a striped blank—or add stain, dye, or paint after cutting to spruce up bland woods. Get creative and take your time; these statement pieces will "hang" around for years to come!

Getting Started

1. Cut the blanks to size, making sure the stock is square. I used solid maple for one pair and glue-ups of redheart and yellowheart for the other. Cover two adjacent sides of each blank with clear packaging tape. Fold each pattern on the centerline, and attach to the tape using spray adhesive. Note: You could also forego the spray adhesive and print your patterns on label paper. Cover the patterns with another layer of clear packaging tape, and drill the holes for the inside cuts.

Cutting and Finishing

2. For each blank, make the inside cuts on one side, then turn the workpiece and make the inside cuts on the adjacent side. Drill a hole for the outside cut on one side of the blank; drilling a hole and cutting the outside, rather than cutting in from the edge, helps keep the blank intact and therefore easier to maneuver. Then, make the first perimeter cut on the side with the drilled hole. Rotate the blank and tape the waste back in place with clear packaging tape. Then, drill an entry hole for the second outside cut and cut the perimeter. Repeat this sequence with the second blank.

3. Separate the earrings; I like to carefully slice into the sides of the waste for ease of removal. Carefully drill a hole in the knob at the top of the pyramid designs; I secured the earring in the scrap to have a flat surface. Sand away any fuzzies with sandpaper and needle files. Take your time and be meticulous. Finish as desired; I dipped each earring in diluted shellac, sanding with a Mac Mop between coats. Add the findings, and they're ready to wear!

MATERIALS

For the Icicle
- ❏ Two maple wood blanks: ¾" (1.9cm) square x 1⅞" (4.8cm) long

For the Pyramid
- ❏ Two yellowheart and/or redheart wood blanks: 1" (2.5cm) square x 1⅞" (4.8cm) long

- ❏ Wood glue (optional)
- ❏ Clear packaging tape
- ❏ Spray adhesive
- ❏ Label paper (optional)
- ❏ Sandpaper, assorted grits
- ❏ Finish, such as clear shellac
- ❏ Wire fishhook findings

TOOLS
- ❏ Band saw
- ❏ Scroll saw with blades: Pegas #3R MGT or similar
- ❏ Drill press with bit: ¹/₁₆" (2mm) diameter
- ❏ Needle files
- ❏ Mac Mop
- ❏ Clamps (optional)

PATTERN LOCATED ON PAGE 112

Songbird in a Birdcage

Capture a bit of spring with compound-cut decorative birdcages

BY SUE MEY

Add a touch of whimsy to your office or living room with a small decorative birdcage, complete with a matching wooden bird. Because large pieces of wood won't fit in a scroll saw, this project relies on you cutting small pieces and gluing them together. The success of the project depends on two factors: precisely cutting or sanding the blanks to size before applying the patterns, and carefully and consistently cutting on the pattern lines. If the clearance on your saw does not allow you to cut the almost 2" (5.1cm) thick material, reduce the size of the pattern slightly, and use the largest wood your saw will accommodate.

MATERIALS

For the Birdcage
❑ Four jelutong or basswood wood blanks: 1⅞" (4.8cm) square x 5¹¹⁄₁₆" (14.5cm) long

For the Bird Body
❑ Jelutong or basswood wood blank: 1" (2.5cm) square x 2³⁄₁₆" (5.6cm) long

For the Bird's Wings
❑ Jelutong or basswood wood blank: 1" (2.5cm) square x 2¹¹⁄₁₆" (2.5cm x 6.8cm) long

- -

❑ Temporary-bond spray adhesive or glue stick
❑ Clear packaging tape
❑ Masking tape or blue painter's tape
❑ Sandpaper
❑ Wood glue
❑ Cyanoacrylate (CA) glue
❑ Clear spray varnish
❑ Thin string or cotton thread
❑ Thin link chain

TOOLS
❑ Scroll saw with blades: #7, #9
❑ Drill press with bits: ¹⁄₃₂" (1mm), ⅛" (3mm) diameter
❑ Table saw (optional)
❑ Disc or belt sander (optional)
❑ Stiff-bristled paintbrush
❑ Clamps
❑ Carving knife (optional)
❑ Rotary tool (optional)
❑ Diagonal pliers
❑ Carving tools of choice (optional)

Using Diagonal Pliers

You may have heard these tools called wire cutters or side cutters. They have diagonal blades on one side, and allow you to easily cut off the extra slats close to the top and bottom, reducing the time spent carving away the extra wood.

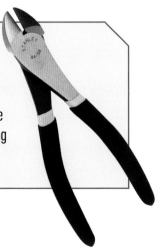

PATTERN
LOCATED ON
PAGE 112

Birdcage: Cutting the Pieces

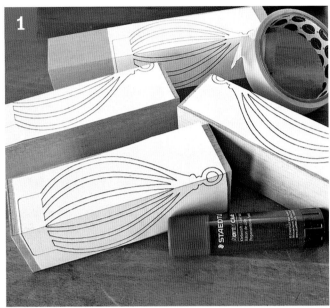

1. Use a table saw to cut the blanks to size. You can also cut them with your saw of choice, and use a disc sander or belt sander to sand the blanks to the exact dimensions. Cover the blanks with masking tape or blue painter's tape. Fold the patterns on the dotted lines, apply adhesive to the backs of the patterns, align the folds with the corners of the blanks, and press the patterns into place.

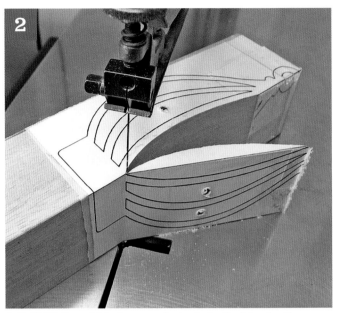

2. Drill ⅛" (3mm) blade-entry holes in both sides for the frets. Using a #9 blade, cut the round opening at the top and the curved edge of one side. For these cuts, saw all the way through the wood but stop just before cutting the paper free; leaving the pattern intact makes it easier to align later.

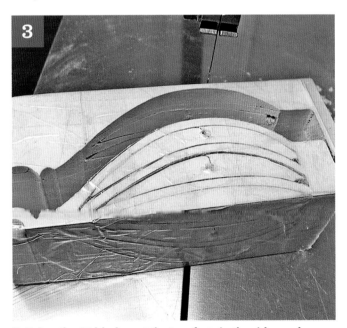

3. Using the #9 blade, cut the two frets in the side you began; then, cut around the perimeter. Vacuum away the dust and tape the pieces back in place. Rotate the blank and cut the second side. Carefully remove the completed birdcage section from the waste, and peel off any remaining pattern or tape.

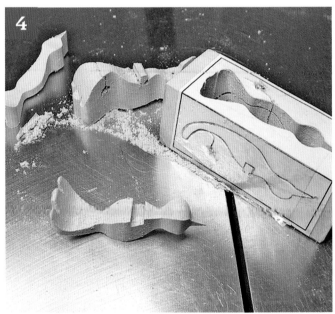

4. Use a #7 blade to cut along one side of the bird pattern. Replace the waste, use clear tape to secure it, and then cut the second side. Use wood glue or cyanoacrylate (CA) glue to attach the wing section to the square mortise in the top of the bird body.

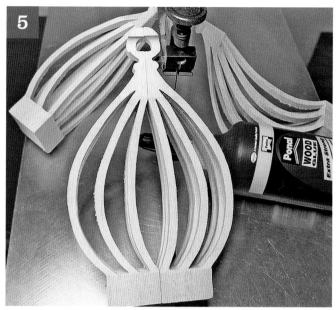

5. Glue and clamp together two pieces (each representing a quarter of the completed birdcage). Make sure the pieces line up nicely. Assemble the other half using the same technique. Do not assemble the two halves yet.

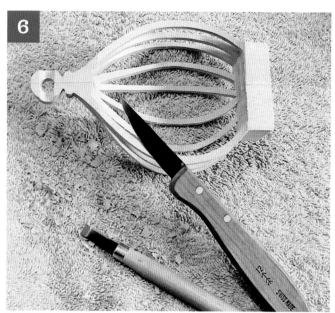

6. To create an opening in the middle of the birdcage, you need to remove the extra slats. I use diagonal pliers to snip the slats as close to the top and bottom as possible, and use carving tools, a knife, or a rotary tool to smooth the inside of the cage. Carve a groove in the top to hold the bird-hanging string.

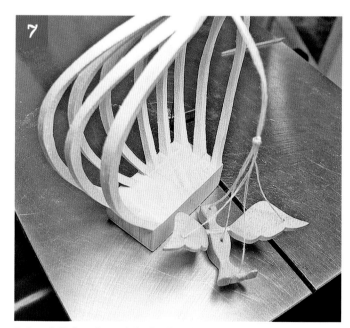

7. Carefully hand-sand the bird and the inside surfaces of the two halves. Remove all of the sanding dust using a stiff-bristled paintbrush. Drill 1/32" (1mm) holes in the head, body, tail, and wings of the bird. Use CA glue to secure strands of cotton thread in the holes. Knot the threads together at the top.

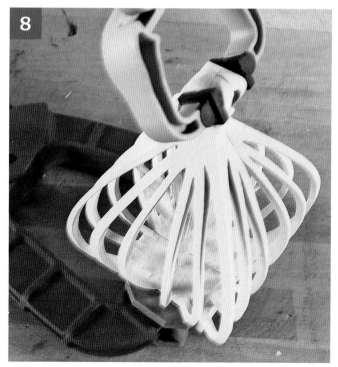

8. Place the thread with the bird attached inside the groove you prepared, and then glue and clamp the two halves together. When the glue has dried, hand-sand the outside surfaces and remove irregularities. Apply several coats of clear spray varnish to the project. Allow the varnish to dry thoroughly between coats, and sand it lightly with 500-grit sandpaper. Attach a thin link chain to the top opening of the birdcage.

Birds of a Feather

Take your skills to new heights with four avian designs

BY SUE MEY

CUT BY JOE PASCUCCI

These bird designs are fun and challenging; take special care on the owl's facial details, the eagle's talons, the hummingbird's beak, and the flamingo's long legs. For the wood blanks, choose pine, spalted maple, aromatic cedar, or walnut.

MATERIALS

- ❏ Wood blanks, as needed: 1½" (3.8cm) square x various heights (see patterns)
- ❏ Clear packaging tape
- ❏ Spray adhesive or glue stick
- ❏ Sandpaper, assorted grits up to 320
- ❏ Wood filler (optional)
- ❏ Finish, such as clear satin spray varnish
- ❏ Small eyelet (optional)
- ❏ Ribbon or thread (optional)

TOOLS

- ❏ Scroll saw with blades: #5, #7, or #9 reverse-tooth
- ❏ Drill press with bit: ⅛" (3mm) diameter
- ❏ Vacuum
- ❏ Rotary tool (optional)
- ❏ Square
- ❏ Stiff-bristled paintbrush
- ❏ Woodburner (optional)

Getting Started

1. Cut the pattern blank to size, making sure that the sides are flat and at a 90-degree angle to each other. Photocopy the pattern, fold it on the centerline, and apply to the back a repositionable glue stick or spray adhesive. Align the fold with the corner of the blank, and press the pattern into place. Use a ⅛" (3mm) bit to drill the blade-entry holes in the flamingo and eagle. Make sure to partially drill the owl's round eyes, in the front view rather than going the whole way through.

2. Select a blade size appropriate for the thickness and hardness of the wood being used. I use a #5 or #7 blade for softer wood like pine, but for something harder, such as maple or walnut, consider a #9.

Cutting and Sanding

3. Cut the first pattern view; go slowly and let the blade do the work. When cutting the flamingo, take extra care under the chin and around the knobby knees. Symmetry is key for the hummingbird's wings, so avoid pushing the workpiece too hard, and stay as close to the line as possible without veering off course. When cutting the eagle, take extra care on the tail feathers.

4. Once done, hold the workpiece and the waste in place and vacuum away the dust. Wrap the entire block (waste and all) in clear packaging tape, rotate the blank 90 degrees, and then cut the second pattern view.

5. Carefully remove the waste wood and sand the piece smooth with 120-grit sandpaper, moving progressively through the grits to 320. Refine the beaks further with a rotary tool, if desired. Remove the sanding dust with a stiff-bristled paintbrush. If you cut the hummingbird, glue the wing piece to the body. For the owl, woodburn the beak lines between the eyes. Once the glue is dry, use wood filler to seal any gaps.

Finishing

6. Apply a finish. I applied several thin coats of clear spray varnish, allowing each coat to dry completely before applying the next. Attach an eyelet to the hummingbird and hang with a ribbon or thread, if desired.

PATTERNS LOCATED ON PAGE 113

Floral Arrangement

These colorful buds will stand the test of time

BY CLAYTON MEYERS

This floral arrangement began as a Valentine's Day gift. Pine accepts dyes well, which makes it suitable to be painted up in Valentine's Day colors. However, less advanced scrollers who still want to apply color can use denser wood varieties, such as maple or birch, for greater stability while cutting. Or use cherry or padauk with a clear finish for a naturally red rose.

PATTERN LOCATED ON PAGES 114-116

MATERIALS

For the Tulip
- ❏ Wood blank: 1½" (3.8cm) square x 9¹³/₁₆" (25cm) long

For the Rose
- ❏ Wood blank: 1½" (3.8cm) square x 7½" (19.1cm) long

For the Lotus
- ❏ Wood blank: 1" (2.5cm) square x 7" (17.8cm) long

For the Vase
- ❏ Wood blank: ¼" (6mm) thick x 2⁹/₁₀" (7.4cm) diameter (small top ring)
- ❏ Wood blank: ¼" (6mm) thick x 3¼" (8.3cm) diameter (large top ring)
- ❏ Wood blank: ¼" (6mm) thick x 3½" (8.9cm) diameter (small bottom ring)
- ❏ Wood blank: ¼" (6mm) thick x 4" (10.2cm) diameter (large bottom ring)

- ❏ Six wood blanks: ³/₁₆" (4.8mm) thick x 1¼" x 5" (3.2cm x 12.7cm) (uprights)
- ❏ Spray adhesive
- ❏ Sandpaper, assorted grits up to 220
- ❏ Clear packaging tape
- ❏ Dyes
- ❏ Rubbing alcohol
- ❏ High-gloss clear spray finish
- ❏ Wood glue
- ❏ Resin (optional)

TOOLS
- ❏ Scroll saw with blades: #3
- ❏ Drill press with bit: ¹/₈" (3mm) diameter
- ❏ Combination square
- ❏ Jeweler's file (optional)
- ❏ Small paintbrush
- ❏ Heat gun (optional)

Getting Started

1. Attach the pattern views to two adjacent sides of the blanks using spray adhesive. Do the same for the vase blank. Use a combination square to verify that the wood blank is perfectly square at all four corners. Drill the blade-entry holes for all the interior cuts on both sides of the blanks. Then drill the entry holes on the appropriate side of the vase blank.

2. Lightly sand the pattern-free sides of the blanks so that they sit flush on your cutting surface. Ensure that your scroll saw blade is perfectly plumb (perpendicular to the table) before you start cutting, as any fluctuation of the blade will cause the piece to look thinner on one side than the other.

Cutting the Flowers

3. Make all the interior cuts for each flower on one side of the blank. Then, rotate the blank 90 degrees and make all the interior cuts on the second side. Stay as close to the pattern lines as possible, cut slowly, and use a fresh blade. Note: While you are making the cuts after rotating 90 degrees, the thickness of the wood will vary depending on what portion of the piece you are cutting through. Avoid exerting too much force, as you can easily overcut the line while traveling into a thinner portion of the blank.

4. After finishing the interior cuts, begin on the outside cuts. Take extra care on the thorns. Make all outside cuts for the first side in one pass, saving the waste pieces for later.

5. Using clear packaging tape, tape the waste pieces to the block exactly as they were before. Rotate the flower 90 degrees, make the outside cuts on the final side, and then remove all the waste wood.

Cutting the Vase

6. The vase is made of 10 individual pieces: two rings for the top, two rings for the base, and six compound-cut uprights that make up the sides. The base and top rim have slots for the uprights to insert into for consistent spacing and strength.

Adding Resin

Instead of coloring the project with dyes, you can add color with a resin fill. If you choose this approach, make all the inside cuts on both sides, remove the waste wood, and clean out any sawdust. Then cover three sides of the blank with clear packaging tape to create a makeshift mold for the resin to fill.

Mix the resin, add a colored pigment of your choice, and pour the mixture into the openings, filling the piece as much as possible. Use a heat gun to pop any bubbles in the resin, and let it cure for several days (check the manufacturer's instructions for specific cure times). Cut the outer profile, sand the exterior, and apply a clear finish. Note: Make sure to wear the appropriate protective gear (a mask, disposable gloves, and goggles) when handling resin.

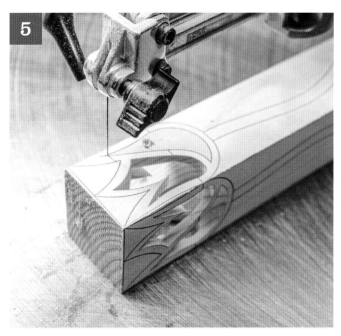

7. Attach the uprights pattern to the blanks, lining up the fold of each with the edge of the wood. Starting with the front view, make the interior cuts (shaded gray on the pattern), and then cut the outside profiles. Tape the waste wood back in place with clear packaging tape, rotate the blank 90 degrees, and cut the side view. Then, cut the rings.

Finishing

8. Sand and finish the pieces to your liking. I smoothed the edges lightly with assorted grits of sandpaper, moving up progressively through the grits to 220. To achieve a vivid color, I used assorted solvent dyes. Mix a very small amount with rubbing alcohol, and then apply it with a small paintbrush. Once dry, apply three coats of a high-gloss polyurethane. Assemble the vase, referring to the assembly drawing at right. Use small amounts of wood glue, and wipe off any squeeze-out immediately.

Majestic Lighthouses

Complete your beach day with these nautical structures

BY SUE MEY

CUT BY JOE PASCUCCI

These lighthouses celebrate those special days spent on the coastline—swooping seagulls, crashing waves, a lighthouse on the horizon. Display one wherever a nautical touch is needed, or show them off in a group as a table decoration, with some beachy pebbles in between. You can leave them natural or make them colorful depending on your preference.

Getting Started

1. Cut the pattern blank to size, making sure that the sides are flat and at a 90-degree angle to each other. Photocopy the pattern, fold it on the centerline, and then apply adhesive to the back with a repositionable glue stick or spray adhesive. Align the fold with the corner of the blank, and press the pattern into place. Use a ⅛" (3mm) bit to drill the blade-entry holes.

2. Select a blade size appropriate for the thickness and type of wood being used. I use a #9 reverse-tooth for softer woods. such as pine, but consider a #12 blade for something harder, such as maple or walnut.

Cutting and Sanding

3. Cut the first pattern view, starting with the interior cuts and moving to the perimeter. Once done, hold the workpiece and the waste in place and vacuum away the dust. Wrap the entire block (waste and all) in clear packaging tape, rotate the blank 90 degrees, and then cut the second pattern view.

4. Carefully remove the waste wood, and sand the piece smooth with 120-grit sandpaper, moving progressively through the grits until you reach 320. You could use a rotary tool to round over the sharp edges, if desired. Remove the sanding dust with a stiff-bristled paintbrush.

Finishing

5. Apply a finish. For a natural look, apply several thin coats of clear spray varnish, allowing each coat to dry completely before applying the next. For painted pieces, use diluted acrylics in your choice of colors. Let dry, and then spray with a clear finish of your choice.

MATERIALS

- ❏ Wood blanks, as needed: 1½" (3.8cm) square x various heights (see patterns)
- ❏ Masking tape
- ❏ Clear packaging tape
- ❏ Spray adhesive or glue stick
- ❏ Sandpaper, assorted grits
- ❏ Finish, such as clear satin spray varnish
- ❏ Acrylic paints (optional)

TOOLS

- ❏ Scroll saw with blades: #9 to #12 reverse-tooth
- ❏ Drill press with bit: ⅛" (3mm) diameter
- ❏ Square (optional)
- ❏ Rotary tool (optional)
- ❏ Vacuum
- ❏ Stiff-bristled paintbrush
- ❏ Paintbrushes (optional)

PATTERN LOCATED ON PAGES 117–118

Giraffe Pair

This power couple is ready to take on the savanna

BY SUE MEY

CUT BY STAFF OF *SCROLL SAW WOODWORKING & CRAFTS*

Social and friendly by nature, giraffes are stunning animals that can be found all over sub-Saharan Africa. They live in groups called "towers" and are the world's tallest mammals. Their long necks evolved to allow them to eat the leaves of high trees, particularly mimosa and acacia. You can use a rotary tool to make the completed shapes more lifelike.

Getting Started

1. Apply masking tape or painter's tape to the workpiece. Photocopy the pattern, and then cut along the perimeter lines for the rectangles. Fold the pattern on the dotted centerline, and then apply spray adhesive or glue stick to the back. Align the fold with the corner of the blank and the bottom with the straight edge of the wood. Press the pattern into place, removing all bubbles.

Cutting and Shaping

2. Make the scroll saw cuts on one side. I suggest a #7 blade for softer wood like pine and a #9 blade for hardwoods. Replace the waste pieces, and wrap clear tape around the blanks to secure them. Rotate the blank 90 degrees and cut the second side. Remove the waste wood.

3. Refine the giraffes' shapes. You can refine the shape of the giraffes using a rotary tool or hand carving tools, and create ossicones (the two protrusions on a giraffe's head) for your animals. To do this, separate the knob on each animal's head, and round over the square edges.

Finishing

4. Sand the pieces by hand until you achieve a smooth finish. Remove all the sanding dust with a stiff-bristled paintbrush. Apply stain or paint, if desired, and allow to dry. Apply several thin coats of clear spray varnish to the giraffe, allowing each coat to dry before applying the next.

MATERIALS

- ❏ 2 pine or basswood wood blanks: 1½" (3.8cm) square x 6" (15.2cm) long
- ❏ Masking tape or painter's tape
- ❏ Clear packaging tape
- ❏ Spray adhesive or glue stick
- ❏ Sandpaper, assorted grits up to 320
- ❏ Wood stain or acrylic paints (optional)
- ❏ Finish, such as clear satin spray varnish

TOOLS

- ❏ Scroll saw with blades: #7 or #9 reverse-tooth
- ❏ Rotary tool with bits or hand carving tools (optional)
- ❏ Paintbrushes
- ❏ Stiff-bristled paintbrush

PATTERN LOCATED ON PAGE 119

Giraffe Pair **43**

Simple Cacti

Populate your favorite ledge or windowsill with a family of low-maintenance plants

BY SUE MEY

CUT BY THE STAFF OF *SCROLL SAW WOODWORKING & CRAFTS*

If you lack a green thumb, cacti might just be the plants for you—especially these! Simple and cute with no internal frets, these designs are excellent for those interested in trying compound cutting for the first time. They're small enough to cut quickly without overwhelming your saw, and all you need to make them shelf-ready are toothpicks and a bit of paint.

MATERIALS

- ❏ Wood blanks, as needed: 1⁵⁄₁₆" (3.3cm) square x various heights (see patterns)
- ❏ Wooden toothpicks
- ❏ Repositionable glue stick
- ❏ Clear packaging tape
- ❏ Sandpaper, assorted grits up to 320
- ❏ Wood glue (optional)
- ❏ Finish, such as clear satin spray varnish
- ❏ Acrylic paints (optional)

TOOLS

- ❏ Scroll saw with blades: #7 reverse tooth
- ❏ Drill press with bit: ¹⁄₁₆" (2mm) diameter
- ❏ Vacuum
- ❏ Square (optional)
- ❏ Stiff-bristled paintbrush
- ❏ Paintbrushes (optional)
- ❏ Pliers
- ❏ Scalpel
- ❏ Tweezers
- ❏ Clamps

PATTERN LOCATED ON PAGE 120

Getting Started

1. Cut the pattern blank to size, making sure that the sides are flat and at a 90-degree angle to each other. Photocopy the pattern, fold it on the centerline, and apply adhesive to the back with a repositionable glue stick. Align the fold with the corner of the blank, and press the pattern into place.

2. Select a blade size appropriate for the thickness and hardness of the wood being used. I used a #7 reverse-tooth blade for cutting the cacti from pine, but consider a #9 for something harder, such as maple or walnut.

Cutting and Scrolling

3. Cut the first pattern view. Once done, hold the workpiece and the waste in place and vacuum away the dust. Wrap the entire block (waste and all) in clear packaging tape, rotate the blank, and cut the second pattern view.

4. Carefully remove the waste wood, and sand the piece with 120-grit sandpaper. Then move up progressively through the grits until you reach 320. Remove the sanding dust with a stiff-bristled paintbrush.

5. Drill the holes for the thorns. Clamp the workpiece to the drill bit table, then carefully lower the drill bit into the cactus at the angle you wish the spine to stand out. Cover the surface of the cactus with as many randomly placed holes as you like. Adjust the depth of the holes based on the thickness of each cactus.

Finishing and Adding the Thorns

6. Apply a finish. For a natural piece, apply several thin coats of clear spray varnish, allowing each coat to dry completely before applying the next. For painted pieces, use acrylics in various shades of green and blue for the top parts and paint the pots as desired.

7. Add the thorns. Cut a handful of toothpicks to size; I used side-cutting pliers, sharpening any pieces that did not naturally come to a point with a scalpel. Insert the toothpicks into the drilled holes with a pair of tweezers. My pieces were tight enough not to need any glue, but you could use small dabs of wood glue, if necessary. Let the glue dry.

Alighting Butterfly

Watch this colorful pollinator emerge from just three little scraps of wood

BY DIANA THOMPSON

CUT BY JOE PASCUCCI

There are few compound-cut subjects more fitting than the butterfly. Think about it. From the outside of the cocoon, it seems like nothing is happening—until the very end, when the elegant insect emerges, defined and complete and in one piece. Precision is key in this project, but once you get the hang of it, you'll be cranking out enough of these critters to fill an entire butterfly house.

MATERIALS

For the Body
- ❏ Maple wood blank: 1½" (3.8cm) square x 3⁷⁄₈" (9.8cm) long

For the Leaf
- ❏ Poplar wood blank: 1½" (3.8cm) square x 3½" (8.9cm) long

For the Wings
- ❏ Purpleheart wood blank: 1½" (3.8cm) square x 3½" (8.9cm) long

- ❏ Spray adhesive
- ❏ Clear packaging tape
- ❏ Sandpaper: 220-grit
- ❏ Wood glue
- ❏ Finish, such as clear semigloss spray lacquer
- ❏ Cloth rags

TOOLS
- ❏ Drill press with bits: assorted small
- ❏ Scroll saw with blades: #5 skip-tooth

1. Attach the body, wing, and leaf patterns to the blanks using spray adhesive. Make sure the fold on the dotted line corresponds with a corner. Note: I included two different wing patterns for this project; you can cut one or both. Drill the blade-entry holes on the wing and leaf blanks.

2. Cut the pieces. I used a #5 skip-tooth blade, but you can adjust blade size depending on your wood selection. Carefully cut the side views first—the leaf outline, the notched part of the butterfly body, and the wing shape. For the wings, cut the inner frets before moving on to the perimeter. Once you've cut each side view, rotate the blank 90 degrees, and wrap it with clear packaging tape to secure the waste wood. Then cut the front views.

3. Remove the pieces from the waste wood. Gently hand-sand with 220-grit sandpaper, and buff each piece with a clean, dry cloth to remove excess dust. Finish as desired; I used a few coats of clear semigloss spray lacquer in order to show off the natural colors of the wood. Glue the wings to the notch on the torso and the torso to the top of the leaf. Let dry and display.

PATTERN LOCATED ON PAGE 121

Alighting Butterfly **47**

Colony of Mushrooms

Scroll a slew of fungi for a favorite ledge or nook

BY SUE MEY

CUT BY THE STAFF OF *SCROLL SAW WOODWORKING & CRAFTS*

Neither plant nor animal, mushrooms belong to the fungi kingdom. There are more than 50,000 species of mushrooms worldwide, and they come in a world of different shapes, colors, and sizes. Since the fruiting bodies of mushrooms have radial symmetry, they are ideal subjects for compound-cutting.

Getting Started

1. Cut the pattern blank to size, making sure that the sides are flat and at a 90-degree angle to each other. Photocopy the pattern, fold it on the centerline, and apply adhesive to the back with a repositionable glue stick or spray adhesive. Align the fold with the corner of the blank, and press the pattern into place. If you are cutting the morel, use a ⅛" (3mm) bit to drill the blade-entry holes. Note: Instead of making the inside cuts for the morel mushroom, you can carve texture on the top using handheld tools, such as a V-tool, gouge, or a router tool with a V-groove bit.

2. Select a blade size appropriate for the thickness and hardness of the wood being used. I use a #7 reverse-tooth blade when I cut the mushrooms from pine, but consider a #9 for something harder, such as maple or walnut.

Cutting and Scrolling

3. Cut the first pattern view. Once done, hold the workpiece and the waste in place and vacuum away the dust. Wrap the entire block (waste and all) in clear packaging tape, rotate the blank, and cut the second pattern view.

4. Carefully remove the waste wood, and sand the piece smooth. Start with 120-grit sandpaper, moving progressively through the grits until you reach 320. Remove the sanding dust with a stiff-bristled paintbrush.

Finishing

5. Apply a finish. For a natural piece, apply several thin coats of clear spray varnish, allowing each coat to dry completely before applying the next. For painted pieces, use thinned acrylics in your choice of colors. Add dots on the mushroom tops in contrasting shades. Let the paint dry, and then spray with a clear finish of your choice.

MATERIALS

- ❏ Basswood or pine wood blanks, as needed: 1½" (3.8cm) square x various heights (see patterns)
- ❏ Clear packaging tape
- ❏ Spray adhesive or glue stick
- ❏ Sandpaper, assorted grits
- ❏ Finish, such as clear satin spray varnish
- ❏ Acrylic paints (optional)

TOOLS

- ❏ Scroll saw with blades: #7 or #9 reverse-tooth
- ❏ Drill press with bit: ⅛" (3mm) diameter
- ❏ Vacuum
- ❏ Square (optional)
- ❏ Stiff-bristled paintbrush
- ❏ Paintbrushes (optional)
- ❏ V-tool, gouge, or rotary tool with a V-groove bit (optional)

PATTERN
LOCATED
ON PAGES
122-124

Later, Alligators

Sharpen your compound-cutting skills with these toothsome alligators that won't bite back

BY AL BAGGETTA

You may have seen these creatures lurking in swampy, wooded areas in the American South, waiting for a meal to come along. The alligator is a unique animal with its armor-plated covering, sharp teeth, and sleek body. They make for great wooden figurines.

MATERIALS

For the Adult Gator

- ❏ Pine or fir wood blank: 1½" (3.8cm) square x 10" (25.4cm) long

For the Baby Gator

- ❏ Pine or fir wood blank: 1¼" (3.2cm) square x 7½" (19.1cm) long

- ❏ Painter's tape
- ❏ Clear packaging tape
- ❏ Glue stick or spray adhesive
- ❏ Sandpaper: 120-grit

- ❏ Clear spray finish
- ❏ Spray paint
- ❏ Black acrylic paint (optional)
- ❏ Toothpicks (optional)

TOOLS

- ❏ Scroll saw with blades: #5 or #7 reverse-tooth
- ❏ Table saw (optional)
- ❏ Drill press with bit: ⅛" (3mm) diameter
- ❏ Sanding mop with 120-grit sandpaper (optional)

PATTERN LOCATED ON PAGE 125

Getting Started

1. Select a soft wood, such as pine or fir. Cover the blank with painter's tape. Then, attach the pattern to the blank with a glue stick or spray adhesive. Make sure the dividing line on the pattern sits perfectly along one edge of the blank so that the pattern covers two adjacent sides of the blank. Drill a blade-entry hole at the tip of the pattern with a ⅛" (3mm) bit.

Cutting

2. Using a #5 or #7 reverse-tooth blade, begin cutting one side of the pattern. The wood is rather thick, so work slowly and don't force the cut by pushing. Let the blade do the work. When you have finished one side, cover the cut sides with clear packaging tape to prevent the waste wood from falling out or moving around.

3. Insert the blade in the uncut side and cut along the pattern. When you have finished the second side, slowly push out the center piece, discarding the end pieces and any scrap wood. Lo and behold, you will have one fierce-looking alligator!

Sanding and Finishing

4. Sand the alligator, rounding over and smoothing out the edges and sharp tail. I used a sanding mop with 120-grit sandpaper, but you can hand-sand, as well. Finish with clear spray to let the woodgrain show, or use regular spray paint in your favorite color. Add the eyes with a toothpick and black acrylic paint, if desired.

Snake Duo

Slice up your blank to reveal the slithering surprise inside

BY AL BAGGETTA

Over the years, the snake has received a lot of bad press. But, as the poet Emily Dickinson describes him, he's just a "narrow fellow in the grass." The compound-cutting method produces a 3D figure from the core of a blank. What's fun is that you won't know what you are going to get until the very end, when the cutting is complete. This method takes a little practice, but once you get the technique down, you will find it easy to do. Here are two patterns—an adult and a baby snake.

MATERIALS

For the Adult Snake
- ❏ Maple, walnut, or mahogany wood blank: 1½" (3.8cm) square x 8³/₈" (21.3cm) long

For the Baby Snake
- ❏ Maple, walnut, or mahogany wood blank: 1½" (3.8cm) square x 5½" (14cm) long

- ❏ Blue painter's tape
- ❏ Clear packaging tape
- ❏ Spray adhesive
- ❏ Sandpaper, 120-grit (optional)
- ❏ Stains, dyes, acrylic paints, and markers, for adding color (optional)
- ❏ Toothpicks
- ❏ Clear spray finish

TOOLS
- ❏ Scroll saw with blades: #5 reverse-tooth
- ❏ Drill press with bit: ¹/₈" (3mm) diameter
- ❏ Sanding mop with 120-grit sandpaper
- ❏ Woodburner with nib (optional)

Getting Started

1. The length of the blank should be longer than the pattern so that you have something to grasp while cutting. Cover two adjacent sides of the blank with blue painter's tape. Attach the pattern views to the surface of the tape using spray adhesive, making sure the grain runs the length of the blank. Then use a ⅛" (3mm) bit to drill a blade-entry hole at one end of the pattern for each of the two sides.

Cutting

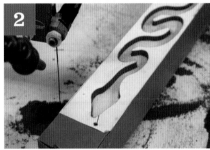

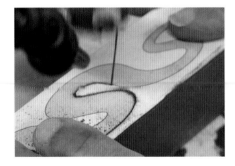

2. Start at the end of the pattern, and weave your blade carefully along the outer edge of the profile. When you finish this first cut, the snake will be two-dimensional and will drop in and out of the blank. Use clear packaging tape to tape the waste back in place. Rotate the blank 90 degrees, and then insert the blade through the blade-entry hole. Cut the second part of the profile the same way you did the first: slowly and carefully. Once you're finished, remove the tape and free the snake from the blank.

Sanding and Finishing

3. Sand and finish the piece to your liking. I used a sanding mop with 120-grit sandpaper, but you can hand-sand, if you prefer. Finish the piece by applying color, if desired. Dip the end of a toothpick into paint to apply tiny eyes; I sometimes woodburn eyes. If you used a fine-figured hardwood, apply several coats of a high-gloss polyurethane for a clear, long-lasting finish.

PATTERN LOCATED ON PAGE 126

Lamppost Light and Jewelry Tree

Combine segments to create large 3D projects

BY SUE MEY

Compound-cut projects are limited to the thickness of wood the scroll saw can cut—usually less than 2½" (6.4cm). I began experimenting with different techniques and developed a method of cutting the project in individual segments, and this project is the result. This lamppost is constructed from four identical quarters that combine to create a project larger than what is normally possible with compound cutting techniques. Be sure to make four copies of the pattern.

MATERIALS

- ❏ Four wood blanks: 1½" (3.8cm) square x 11½" (3.8cm x 29.2cm) long

For the Shaker Pegs

- ❏ Wood blanks: ³/₈" (10mm) diameter x 2⁷/₁₆" (6.2cm) long

For the Light

- ❏ Light bulb holder
- ❏ Light bulb
- ❏ 16" (40.6cm) two-core insulated cable with battery pack and switch
- ❏ 9-volt battery
- ❏ Small V-tool and straight chisel or rotary power carver

- ❏ Masking tape
- ❏ Clear packaging tape
- ❏ Temporary-bond spray adhesive or glue stick
- ❏ Sandpaper
- ❏ Wood glue

- ❏ Cyanoacrylate (CA) glue
- ❏ Deep-penetrating liquid furniture wax or Danish oil
- ❏ Clear spray varnish

TOOLS

- ❏ Scroll saw with blades: #9 skip-tooth or blades of choice
- ❏ Drill press with bit: ³/₈" (10mm) diameter
- ❏ Table saw (optional)
- ❏ Sanders: disc or belt (optional)
- ❏ Stiff-bristled paintbrush
- ❏ Medium-size artist's paintbrush
- ❏ Lint-free cloth
- ❏ Damp rag
- ❏ Clamps

Preparing the Stock

1. Cut the pieces slightly oversized on a scroll saw. Then, use a disc or belt sander to sand the pieces to 1½" (3.8cm) by 1½" (3.8cm) x 11½" (29.2cm). A table saw can also be used to cut the pieces to the exact dimensions.

2. Transfer the patterns to the stock. You need four copies of the pattern for each project. Cover the surfaces of the wood with masking tape. Fold the patterns on the dotted centerline, and attach them to the wood.

PATTERN LOCATED ON PAGE 127

Let There Be Light

The project can be constructed for use as a jewelry stand or a night light. I use a torch fitting and globe with thin two-core cable powered by a 9-volt battery for my lamp, but it is also possible to use small LED lights and watch batteries or a plug-in type lamp. The lighted version is a safe alternative to the traditional candles placed in windows. Adjust the size of the pattern to fit a model railroad or Christmas village display.

Making the Cuts

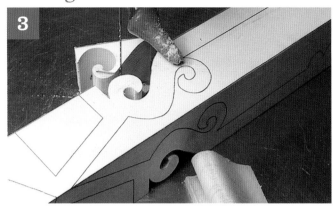

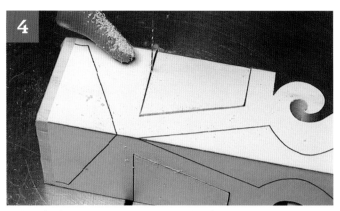

3. Use a #9 skip-tooth blade to cut the curvy decoration on the inside edge of all four pieces (on the side with the opening for the lamp). Cut this area on both sides of the pieces and keep the waste.

4. Cut the lamp opening on one side of the pattern. Use a vacuum to remove the dust and then tape the waste back in place. Cut the lamp opening on the other side and tape all of the waste pieces back in place.

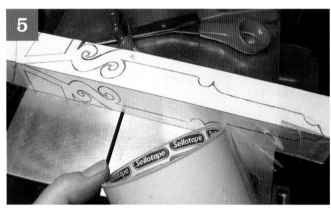

5. Cut in from the outside edge to achieve sharp corners. Make the long cut on one side and then cut the top of the lamp. Secure the waste back in place with clear packaging tape. Cut the other side.

6. Carefully remove the waste pieces, pattern, and tape. Remove the burrs from the cuts and hand sand the pieces with 220-grit sandpaper. Remove the sanding dust with a stiff-bristled paintbrush.

Assembling the Pieces

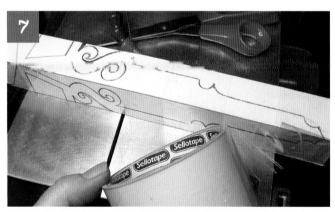

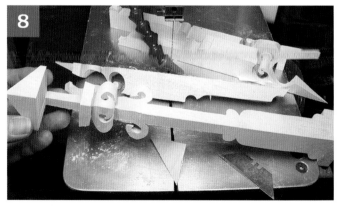

7. Dry-fit the pieces to make sure you have a good fit and make any adjustments necessary. Join the four quarters of the lamppost into two pairs with wood glue and clamps. Remove any glue squeeze out with a damp rag.

8. Add the light (version A). Carve a channel to accommodate the electrical wire with a small V-tool or rotary power carver. Glue the wire and light bulb holder to one half of the assembly with cyanoacrylate (CA) glue. If using an LED light, carve a recess to accommodate the battery, resistor, and LED.

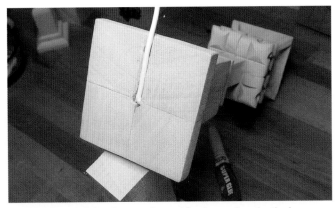

9. Apply wood glue to the other half of the lamppost and clamp it in position overnight. Carve a channel for the cord under the lamp base with a V-tool or rotary power carver. Secure the cord to the base with CA glue. Attach the cord to the battery pack if required.

10. Assemble the jewelry stand (version B). The jewelry stand is assembled the same way as the lighted lamppost, except no lighting hardware is installed. After the glue dries, drill a ⅜" (10mm) diameter hole through the center of the stand just below the curvy part. Glue Shaker pegs in both sides of the hole.

11. Smooth the glue joints with sandpaper. Apply deep-penetrating furniture wax or Danish oil with a medium-sized artist's brush. When dry, wipe the lamp down with a dry lint-free cloth to remove any residue. Apply several coats of clear spray varnish. Allow the varnish to dry thoroughly between coats and sand it lightly between coats with fine-grit sandpaper.

Autumn Leaves

Backfill these beauties with tinted epoxy for an explosion of colors and contours

BY CLAYTON MEYERS

The compound scroll work in this design is simple and easy to execute, while the epoxy backfill adds another layer of color—especially on sunny days. Unlike many other compound scrolling patterns, this project only requires a single view, placed on one side of the blank. You'll draw on the second view later (or attach it), based on your preference. Attach the patterns to their respective blanks with repositionable spray adhesive. Then, using a drill press, drill pilot holes in all of the inside cut areas.

MATERIALS

- ❑ Cherry wood blanks, as needed: 1½" (3.8cm) square x various lengths (see the patterns)
- ❑ Spray adhesive
- ❑ Clear packaging tape
- ❑ Sandpaper, assorted grits up to 500
- ❑ Epoxy resin, such as Alumilite Clear Cast
- ❑ Resin dye, such as Miraclekoo
- ❑ High-gloss clear acrylic spray finish
- ❑ Decorative thread (optional)
- ❑ Paper cups, for mixing
- ❑ Wooden stirrer

TOOLS

- ❑ Scroll saw with blades: #5 reverse-tooth
- ❑ Drill press with bits: ⅛" (3mm) diameter, ¹⁄₃₂" (1mm) (optional)
- ❑ Compressed air can
- ❑ Hot air gun or blowtorch
- ❑ Eye dropper or syringe (optional)

Making the Leaves

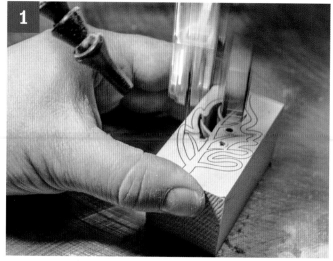

1. Cut out all inside areas on the leaves. Use a scroll saw. Blow out excess sawdust using a can of compressed air. After the first round of scrolling, you will use the workpiece as a mold for the epoxy pour, so any residual dust will float inside the epoxy while it is setting, making for a cloudy appearance. Place a few layers of packaging tape along the bottom side of the blank to create a tight seal.

2. Prepare the epoxy. I used a thick-pour two-part acrylic epoxy. Alumilite Amazing Clear Cast casting resin works well, as do most tabletop epoxy resins. Mix the epoxy carefully according to the manufacturer's instructions; being off on your measurements in one direction or the other can cause the epoxy not to harden fully. Once the epoxy is fully mixed, add dye to your liking. I used a transparent resin colorant meant for use in UV light. This ensures the colors will last even after hanging regularly in the sunlight.

PATTERN
LOCATED ON
PAGE 127

3. Pour the epoxy into the leaf block. Do this slowly, making sure not to trap large air bubbles; a syringe or eye dropper can be helpful here. Overfill it so the epoxy domes slightly over the top surface. Doing this will help counteract shrinkage as the epoxy cures. Use a small blowtorch or hot air gun to pop any bubbles that rise to the surface. Allow the epoxy to cure for two to three days. Even if the surface feels dry and hard after sitting overnight, the inside will need longer to set.

4. Cut the side profiles. Attach the provided side view pattern to the block, or draw several wavy lines along one of the blank sides like I did. Cut along these lines to create several curved slices. Stack them back in order, and then tape them together (along with the waste wood) to create the original block shape. Use clear packaging tape.

5. Make the final cuts. Flip the block 90 degrees, and cut the perimeter of the front leaf view. Remove the leaf slices and discard the waste wood. If you wish to hang the leaves, drill ⅟₃₂" (1mm) holes where indicated on the stems, and display using thin lengths of decorative thread.

Sanding and Finishing

6. After you cut through the epoxy on the scroll saw, some portions will look scratched and white. Hand-sand the surfaces of the leaves to eliminate as many visible scratches as possible, working up progressively through the grits to 500. Once you are happy with them, apply several coats of a clear, high gloss acrylic spray to both sides. The finish will help to fill in small, fine scratches and give the epoxy a glassy look.

Gilded Angel

A simple elevation of a standard angel shape

BY DIANA THOMPSON AND MAC SIMMONS

The leafing technique used in this project can be applied to any of your scrolled projects to increase their appeal. For you professional or semi-professional crafters out there, that means you can boost your selling price.

Cutting and Assembly

1. Cut out the patterns around the rectangle and fold along the dashed line. Apply temporary bond spray adhesive to the patterns' back sides, and wrap them around two sides of the wood. If you prefer to use softwoods, use as sugar pine, white pine, or basswood. If you use hardwoods, you'll find that they're easier to cut if clear packaging tape is applied before adhering the pattern.

2. Cut the left side first in one continuous line. I like to use a #5 single or skip-tooth blade. You can use the #5 to make all of the cuts. Allowing the figure to rest naturally in the block, pinch it in two places and use cellophane tape to keep the pieces together. Cut the right side in one continuous line.

3. Glue the wings into the notch on the back of the body. Apply a wood sealer to each piece before the final assembly for easier working. Use toothpicks to hold the wing kerfs open until the sealer dries. After the sealer dries, do the final sanding and assembly. Fine-grit sandpaper works best. At this point, you're ready to gild your angel.

Gild the Angel

4. Apply masking tape to the wings. Make sure you cover them completely. Use a poly sponge brush to apply a coat of polyurethane to the body and allow it to get tacky. The polyurethane serves as sizing, the material to which the leaf material will adhere.

5. With sharp scissors, cut a sheet of the silver leaf into four strips to cover the body. Pick up each silver leaf with your thumb and forefinger, and lay it on the front of the body. With the flat bristle brush, lightly tamp down the leaf. Do the same for the back, then do the two sides. Allow the sizing to dry for several hours.

6. Use the flat brush to lightly fan off the excess leaf. Save the pieces that fall off to patch missing spots. If any leaf is missing, apply a little size and patch it with a small piece of leaf. Tap it down, allow it to dry, and fan off any excess. Use dental floss to clean out the cut lines.

7. Apply a coat of polyurethane and allow it to dry. This will seal and protect the silver gilding on the body while you're handling the angel. Remove the tape from the wings, and apply new tape on the body near the wings. This will prevent the sizing and gold from getting on the body near the wings. Apply gold leafing to the wings. Repeat the gilding process, substituting gold for silver leaf. Cut a sheet of gold leaf into quarters. Apply two sheets to the front and two to the back.

8. Apply a few more coats of polyurethane. These will help to preserve and protect the gilded angel.

PATTERN LOCATED ON PAGE 128

MATERIALS

- ❏ Wood blank: 1½" (3.8cm) square x 8" (20.3cm) long
- ❏ Spray adhesive
- ❏ ¾" (19mm) cellophane masking tape
- ❏ Wood glue
- ❏ Wood sealer
- ❏ Sandpaper, 220-grit or finer
- ❏ Polyurethane
- ❏ Book of gold and silver leaf
- ❏ Dental floss
- ❏ Clear packaging tape (optional)
- ❏ Toothpicks

TOOLS

- ❏ Scroll saw with blades: #5 single or skip-tooth
- ❏ Scissors
- ❏ Poly sponge brush
- ❏ Flat bristle brush

Spinning Dreidel

Celebrate the Festival of Lights with a homemade take

BY AL BAGGETTA

The dreidel is a spinning top, usually made from wood or metal and beloved as a children's game during Hanukkah. With a little scrap wood, some glue, and a scroll saw, you can easily compound-cut your own!

MATERIALS

- ❏ Fir or padauk wood blank: 1½" (3.8cm) square x 4" (10.2cm) long
- ❏ Blue painter's tape
- ❏ Clear packaging tape
- ❏ Spray adhesive
- ❏ Sandpaper, 120-grit
- ❏ Tack cloth
- ❏ Wood glue
- ❏ Semigloss clear spray finish

TOOLS

- ❏ Scroll saw with blades: #5 to #7 reverse-tooth
- ❏ Table saw
- ❏ Drill press with bit: ¼" (6mm) diameter (optional)
- ❏ Sanding mop (optional)
- ❏ Scissors

Getting Started

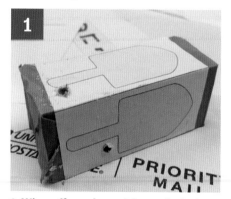

1. Wipe off sawdust with a tack cloth and cover two adjacent long sides of the blank with painter's tape. Fold the pattern along the dotted line, coat the back with spray adhesive, and apply to the surface of the tape, ensuring that the seam corresponds perfectly with a corner of the blank. If desired, use a ¼" (6mm) drill bit to drill the blade-entry holes on both sides of the blank for ease of cutting.

Cutting the Body

2. Using a scroll saw and a #5 reverse-tooth blade, cut along the edges of the dreidel on one side of the blank. Take your time and let the blade do the work; pushing too hard will distort the dreidel's shape. When you are done, place a piece of clear packaging tape over both cut sides, firmly smoothing the tape so that the internal cut piece can't move around. Now, flip the blank 90 degrees and cut the second side. Remove the waste wood to reveal the completed piece. Sand the dreidel with 120-grit sandpaper, and then switch to a sanding mop to smooth the surfaces and round the corners.

Adding the Symbols

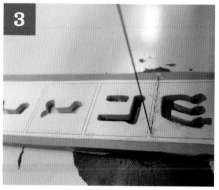

3. Next, make the play symbols. You can do this in three different ways: a) cut each symbol from ⅛" (3mm) plywood, with the sides as waste wood; b) cut each side from ⅛" (3mm) plywood, with the symbols as waste wood; or c) photocopy the shape of each side and symbol, cut them out with scissors, and glue them to the wood. If you chose option (a) or (b), apply the pattern to the plywood using painter's tape and spray adhesive. Then, carefully cut each piece on the scroll saw. Remove the patterns, hand-sand the pieces, and glue them to the main dreidel body. For rich hardwoods, I recommend a clear spray finish; for plain woods, I recommend acrylic paints.

PATTERN LOCATED ON PAGE 128

How to Play the Dreidel Game

The dreidel is more than just a top. On each of the four sides is a Hebrew symbol, an instruction for the game play. Children use common items like nuts, beans, stones, or coins as game pieces (no heavy wagering here). So can you.

Each player puts a game piece in a central cup. Players then take turns spinning the dreidel. The side showing up when the top stops spinning determines the action for that player. The NUN gets nothing. The GIMMEL gives the entire pot to the player. If HAY is showing, the player gets half the pot. If the player gets SHIN, he or she must put a playing piece into the pot. The players around the circle play until only one person with tokens remains.

Spinning Dreidel **63**

Natural Barrettes

Make beautiful accessories to get hair under control

BY MICHELLE MARTIN

Many barrettes available in stores appear to be made from beautifully polished wood, but are actually molded plastic with a painted or laminated woodgrain effect. You can craft your own barrettes using scrap wood or beautifully figured stock. Use natural knots to highlight the design or embellish the barrettes with carefully placed fretwork designs.

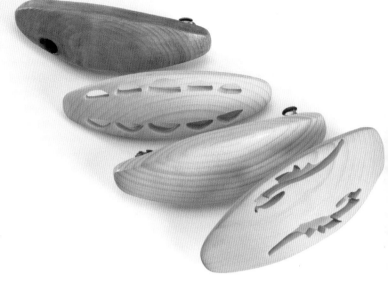

1. Make certain your blade is square to the table. Fold the pattern along the dotted line, and attach it to the blank with spray adhesive. Cover the pattern with clear packaging tape.

2. If you are incorporating a fretwork design, cut that portion first. Cut one side of the pattern, tape the section in place, then cut the other side. Shape the bottom curve of the barrette to accommodate the clasp mechanism. Sand and smooth the curve of the barrette with progressively finer grit of sandpaper.

3. Check the fit of the barrette mechanism. Not every mechanism is the same. Shape the bottom contour to fit your hardware if necessary. Disassemble the barrette mechanism, and attach the back part of the mechanism to the wood with polyurethane or cyanoacrylate (CA) glue. If you use polyurethane glue, use a rag to protect the wood while you clamp the back of the mechanism in place. When the glue is dry, apply your finish of choice. I use polyurethane.

Sharp Blades

Cut slowly and change blades often. When you're cutting through thick hardwoods on a scroll saw, the first sign of a dull blade may be that the wood is starting to burn—so stay vigilant!

MATERIALS
- ❏ Wood blanks, as needed: 1¼" (3.2cm) thick x 1½" x 4½" (3.8 x 11.4cm)

For the Barrette Backing
- ❏ Metal backer: 3¾ (9.5cm) long

- ❏ Spray adhesive
- ❏ Sandpaper, assorted grits up to 220
- ❏ Polyurethane glue or cyanoacrylate (CA) glue
- ❏ Finish, such as water-based clear polyurethane (optional)
- ❏ Clean rags

TOOLS
- ❏ Scroll saw with blades: .018" Olson Thick Wood hooked-tooth or blade of choice
- ❏ Drill press with bit: small (if cutting fretwork design)
- ❏ Clamps (optional)
- ❏ Paintbrushes, foam brushes, or rags, to apply the finish

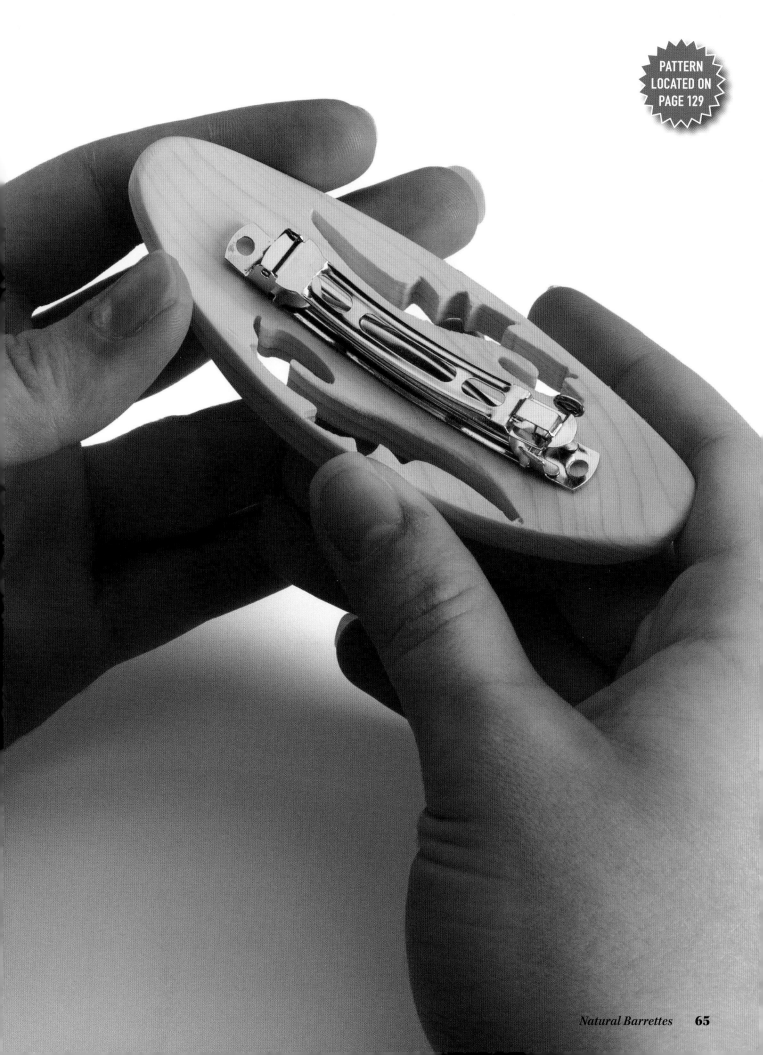

PATTERN
LOCATED ON
PAGE 129

Santa's Reindeer & Sleigh

Dasher, Dancer, and the rest bring presents to the deserving

BY DAVE VAN ESS

Going to a Christmas party? Bring a special gift for your deer friends. When they ask if you made it, tell them it was lumber only hours ago—that never fails to impress. You can cut most of the project using about 3' (91.4cm) of a standard 1x2. This simple reindeer-and-sleigh set is small enough to sit on a ledge or shelf. I used redwood.

PATTERN LOCATED ON PAGE 129

Add different noses for varied looks!

Getting Started

1. Attach the patterns and cut the blanks. Use a ruler to divide the Reindeer and Sleigh Body Center wood blank into 10 identical blocks, ¾" (1.9cm) x 1½" (3.8cm) x 2½" (6.4cm). Nine will be used to make the reindeer and one will be used for the body of the sleigh. Cut the individual blocks on a band or scroll saw and remove any sawdust. Attach the remaining patterns to the thinner wood as specified. For each reindeer, attach the pattern to two adjacent sides of the block, and cover it with packaging tape to reduce burns.

Making the Reindeer

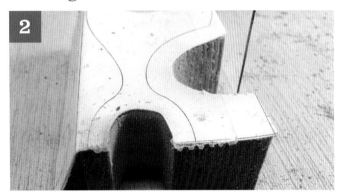 

2. Cut just the dotted lines on the front view of each reindeer. Then, remove the scrap. Turn the blank so the second side of the pattern faces up, and then cut the side view. With the scrap piece held in place, return to the front view and cut the remaining lines. Remove all waste wood and gently sand each reindeer with 220-grit sandpaper.

Making the Sleigh

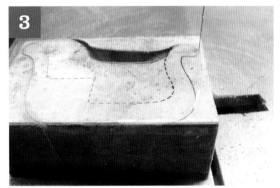 

4. Take one of the ¼" (6mm) thick pieces, attach the runner pattern with spray adhesive, and cut the runners. Remove any fuzzies, glue them to the bottom of the sleigh, and let it dry.

3. The sleigh blank is a stack made of a ¾" (1.9cm) thick piece, sandwiched between two ⅛" (3mm) thick pieces. Tape the stack together with clear packaging tape, attach the pattern with spray adhesive, cover with more packaging tape, and cut the sleigh outline. Disassemble, transfer the pattern to the middle piece, and cut the sleigh interior (indicated by a dashed line on the pattern). Remove any sawdust and glue the pieces together; I used wood glue, as it dries quickly. Once it's dry, sand with 220-grit sandpaper.

Making Santa

5. Cut out the Santa. The Santa blank is a ¼" (6mm) thick piece sandwiched between two ⅛" (3mm) thick pieces. Tape the stack together with clear packaging tape, attach the pattern with spray adhesive, and cut the Santa outline. Trim the head off the two outer pieces and the arms and legs off the center piece. As with the sleigh, glue the pieces together and sand with 220-grit sandpaper.

Finishing

6. Apply a finish. Since I used a rich redwood for my version, I warmed up the color slightly with natural Danish oil, but you could also use clear spray lacquer or an oil-based stain.

For the Home

PATTERN LOCATED ON PAGE 131

Citrus Glass Charms

Top off your beverage with a zesty resin accent

BY CLAYTON MEYERS

These wooden citrus coins will never go bad and can be used to garnish your glassware for a little extra flair. Leave them on the glasses while they're stored in the bar cart to add color to your serving space. They're also a fun way to keep track of whose drink is whose at get-togethers. This project mixes beginner-level compound scrolling with resin work. By using the scroll saw, you can cut voids in the wood blank that the colored epoxy will fill. Then, simply cut it again on the scroll saw to reveal the final shape.

MATERIALS

- ❏ Wood blank: 1½" (3.8cm) square x 10" (25.4cm) long
- ❏ Spray adhesive
- ❏ Clear packaging tape
- ❏ 4 to 6 oz. resin
- ❏ Transparent resin dyes
- ❏ Sandpaper, assorted grits up to 320 (optional)
- ❏ High-gloss finish, such as clear acrylic or polyurethane spray paint
- ❏ Paper towels

TOOLS

- ❏ Band saw (optional)
- ❏ Scroll saw with blades: #5
- ❏ Combination square
- ❏ Drill press with bit: ⅛" (3mm) diameter
- ❏ Hot glue gun
- ❏ Sanders: belt, disc, or orbital

70   3D Scroll Saw Projects

Creating the Mold

1. Make sure your scroll saw blade is perpendicular (90 degrees) to the saw table.
After that, use a small combination square to ensure your wood blank is square

2. Place the workpiece on a large piece of scrap wood or cardboard, and coat two sides of the wood blank with spray adhesive. Don't be stingy here. If you use too much, it's okay, but if you don't use enough, your pattern will fall off.

3. Fold the pattern along the dotted line and apply it to the blank. Make sure the fold lines up with the corner of the wood, adjacent to the sides that are coated with spray adhesive. Press gently along the length of the pattern with a paper towel to flatten it and press out any extra glue. Note: The patterns will be cut away when making the final cuts.

4. Once the adhesive has dried, drill ⅛" (3mm) diameter pilot holes in all shaded areas of the pattern. The shaded areas are where you'll pour the resin later.

5. Use a scroll saw with a #5 standard blade to remove the shaded areas on the pattern. For one of the larger orange slices, you will need to remove the slice from the blank first, and then cut out the shaded area. If desired, seal the woodgrain inside the resin cuts with a clear acrylic or polyurethane spray paint or a small batch (1 oz or less) of epoxy to help eliminate any color bleeding through the grain.

6. Use clear packaging tape to reattach the one loose orange slice. Also, use the packaging tape to seal off the bottom and sides of the blank. This will create the "mold" for where the resin will be poured.

7. Use a hot glue gun to create a dam around each slice. This will allow you to overfill the mold to account for the resin shrinking and soaking into the grain while it hardens. It will also help keep the different colors from spilling over between slices.

Adding the Resin

8. Mix a batch of approximately 4 to 6 ounces of deep-pour resin. Note: For specific ratios, refer to the instructions on the container of resin. Divide the mixed resin into four different cups, one for each of the shapes. Add transparent dye to each of the cups to achieve the desired color. I used two different shades of green and orange for these, though the differences are subtle.

9. Slowly pour the colored resin into each of the openings. It's easiest to pour the resin down the side of a thin stick. This lets you more easily control where the resin is going. Slightly overfill the cutouts until the resin contacts the hot glue.

10. Allow 48 to 72 hours for the resin to fully harden. Then, remove the excess tape and scrape off the hot glue dams.

11. Where a line does not exist to cut, cut along where the colored resin meets the wood. Be sure to use a respiratory mask and goggles when working with resin.

Finishing the Project

12. Sand each of the shapes down to the line (or resin). For this, use a disc sander to achieve that perfect profile.

13. Slice the fruit. For this step, you can use either a scroll saw or band saw. A scroll saw can be used by taping the pieces back to the blank and cutting along the straight lines of the pattern. I used a band saw, so I could set up a fence and quickly cut each of the slices.

14. Sand the workpieces. Start the sanding process by using a belt sander to remove any blade marks from each slice. Then, move to a finer grit sandpaper on an orbital sander. You can use standard sandpaper if a power sander is not available; it will take a bit longer, though. Sand up to 320 grit for a super smooth surface. If you're not very experienced using powered sanders, it's best to sand by hand for this step. Again, wear a mask.

15. Apply the finish. For a durable shine, use a high-gloss acrylic spray paint to finish these off. Lay the slices out on small stands to prevent them from sticking to the table. Apply several coats to each side, allowing each coat to dry fully before applying the next.

Air Plant Holders

Compound-cut cool cubbies hold these popular plants in style

BY SUE MEY

CUT BY ROLF BEUTTENMULLER

Exotic air plants can be tucked into all kinds of cool containers. Show off your scrolling skills by making custom wooden holders for these popular plants. Because large pieces of wood won't fit in a scroll saw, I cut four smaller pieces and glued them together into one large piece.

MATERIALS

- ❏ 4 wood blanks: $1\frac{7}{8}$" (4.8cm) square x various lengths (see the patterns)
- ❏ Masking tape or blue painter's tape
- ❏ Clear packaging tape
- ❏ Spray adhesive or glue stick
- ❏ Sandpaper
- ❏ Wood glue
- ❏ Waterproof adhesive
- ❏ Waterproof finish, such as clear spray varnish
- ❏ Small screw eyes or screw bolts
- ❏ Rubber bands (optional)
- ❏ String or cord
- ❏ Telephone wire or floral wire

TOOLS

- ❏ Table saw or saw of choice
- ❏ Sanders: disc or belt
- ❏ Scroll saw with blades: #9 skip-tooth
- ❏ Drill press with bits: $\frac{1}{8}$" (3mm) twist, 2" (51mm) diameter Forstner
- ❏ Clamps
- ❏ Vacuum
- ❏ Punch or awl
- ❏ Holding jig
- ❏ Stiff-bristled paintbrush

Getting Started

1. Make four copies of each pattern. Use a table saw to cut the blanks to size. You can also cut them with a saw of your choice, and use a disc sander or belt sander to sand the blanks to the exact dimensions. Cover the blanks with masking tape or blue painter's tape. Fold the patterns on the centerlines, apply adhesive to the backs of the patterns, align the folds with the corners of the blanks, and press the patterns into place.

Making the Holders

2. Drill ⅛" (3mm) blade-entry holes in both sides for the frets (where applicable). Using a #9 blade, cut the frets on one side, and then cut the perimeter. Saw all the way through the wood, but stop just before cutting the paper free, leaving the pattern intact, which makes it easier to cut the other side. Vacuum away the dust, and tape the waste pieces back in place. Rotate the blank and cut the second side. Carefully remove the completed section from the waste, and peel off any remaining pattern or tape. After making the final cuts, save the outer waste pieces.

3. Carefully match the outer waste pieces and the inner pieces. This will give you square sides to clamp to; rubber bands work well as clamps. Glue and clamp together two pieces, each representing a quarter of the completed project. Make sure the pieces line up nicely. Use great care not to get any glue on the outer pieces. Assemble the other half using the same technique. Allow the glue to dry. Then, glue and clamp the two halves together. When the glue has dried, remove clamps or rubber bands, and put aside the outer waste pieces to be used later when drilling. Hand-sand the outside surfaces and remove any irregularities.

Drilling the Plant Openings

4. Drill the openings for the plants where indicated on the patterns (if applicable). Match the outer waste—this will give you square sides to hold on to while drilling (although placing the project in a holding jig for drilling is still recommended). Use a drill press for this step. It's challenging and unsafe to drill a straight hole with a Forstner bit with a handheld drill.

PATTERN LOCATED ON PAGES 130–131

5. Make sure the drill press table and the drill bit are perpendicular, both side to side and front to back. Set the drill to the slowest possible speed. Flatten both the top and bottom of the project with a belt or disc sander. Mark the center of the hole with a punch or awl. For some projects, drilling to the proper depth may require an extension for the Forstner bit. Before adding the extension, drill to the maximum depth possible with a standard bit. Drill in ½" (13mm) increments. After each increment, back the bit completely out of the work piece and remove all wood shavings and dust before resuming. Soften the drilled edges with sandpaper, if needed.

Sealing the Project

6. Apply several thin coats of clear spray varnish, or a finish of your choice, to seal the wood. Remember, these holders will be getting wet, so choose a waterproof finish. For hanging holders without a fret opening at the top, insert screw eyes or screw bolts to thread a string or cord through.

Adding the Air Plants

7. Arrange an air plant in the holder. Many look very nice just sitting or hanging in the holder with no mounting at all and can be removed from the holder for watering. To secure a plant in the upside-down holders, choose a strong, waterproof adhesive that is colorless, extremely strong, waterproof, and nontoxic to plants. Apply a small amount of adhesive near the base of the plant, but not on the bottom. Avoid covering the area where the roots form. Using soft, coated wire, such as telephone wire or floral wire, tie the plant securely in place until the adhesive sets. In case of secured plants, use a waterproof varnish for the holder, so you can spray the plants with water.

Picnic Lanterns

Compound-cut tiny tealight holders for your next outdoor gathering

BY SUE MEY

CUT BY JOE PASCUCCI

Sized for battery-operated tealights, these lanterns go great with garden dinners alfresco, evening picnics, or backyard campouts. Cut them from a small piece of 2" (5.1cm) square wood, or laminate two or three pieces of thinner wood to obtain the thickness required. You could also glue up the blank using thin strips of contrasting wood for a more varied appearance.

MATERIALS

- ❏ 2 mahogany or basswood wood blanks: 2" (5.1cm) square x 5½" (14cm) long
- ❏ Masking tape
- ❏ Clear packaging tape
- ❏ Spray adhesive
- ❏ Sandpaper, assorted grits up to 320
- ❏ Clear gloss and/or satin finish
- ❏ Metal jump ring or colored ribbon
- ❏ 2 battery-operated tealight candles

TOOLS

- ❏ Drill press with bit: ⅛" (3mm) diameter
- ❏ Scroll saw with blades: #7, #9, or #12 reverse-tooth
- ❏ Scraper blade (optional)
- ❏ Needle files (optional)
- ❏ Stiff-bristled paintbrush

Prepping and Cutting

1. Prep the blanks for cutting. For straight blade-entry holes and neat inside cuts, the blanks must have perfectly straight 90-degree angled edges. Cover the blanks with masking tape. Fold the patterns on the dotted center lines, and attach them to the blanks with spray adhesive. Drill the blade-entry holes with a ⅛" (3mm) bit. Remove the rough edges with sandpaper or a scraper blade, so the blank sits flat on the saw table. .

2. Make the inside cuts. I use a #7 reverse-tooth blade for soft woods and a #9 or #12 blade for laminated hardwood blanks. Adjust the blade size and type depending on your preference and the type of wood used. Make the interior cut(s) on one side and remove the waste; then turn the blank 90 degrees and make the interior cut(s) on the adjoining side.

3. Cut the entire perimeter on one side of the blank. Hold the work piece and waste in place while you wrap clear packaging tape around the blank. Rotate the blank 90 degrees, and cut the perimeter of the work piece on the second side. Carefully remove the waste wood.

Sanding and Finishing

4. Sand the project by hand, moving up progressively through the grits to 320. Use needle files to smooth inner edges, if necessary. Remove the sanding dust with a stiff-bristled paintbrush. Finish as desired; I applied two to three coats of a clear gloss spray finish, sanding between coats. Follow up with a final thin coat of satin or gloss.

5. Insert a colored ribbon or jump ring through the top opening of the hanging lantern. Place a battery-operated tea light in the lantern and display as desired.

PATTERN LOCATED ON PAGE 133

Garden Lanterns

Combine compound-cut sections to make festive tea light lanterns

BY SUE MEY

CUT BY NORM NICHOLS

These lanterns, which are nearly 4" (10.2cm) wide and 4" (10.2cm) thick—far bigger than a standard compound-cut design—are made by gluing together two quarters at a time, and then gluing the two halves together. Or you can also glue all four quarters at one time. If the clearance on your saw does not allow you to cut 2" (5.1cm) thick material, reduce the size of the patterns slightly and use the largest wood that your saw will accommodate.

MATERIALS

- ❑ 4 wood blanks: 2" (5.1cm) thick x 2" x 7¼" (5.1 x 18.4cm)
- ❑ Blue painter's tape
- ❑ Clear packaging tape
- ❑ Spray adhesive
- ❑ Sandpaper, assorted grits up to 500
- ❑ Wood glue
- ❑ Clear finish, such as clear lacquer
- ❑ Clean rags
- ❑ Rubber bands (optional)

TOOLS

- ❑ Scroll saw with blades: #9 skip reverse-tooth
- ❑ Drill press with bit: ⅛" (3mm) diameter
- ❑ Table saw or choice of saw
- ❑ Disc or belt sander (optional)
- ❑ Stiff-bristled paintbrush
- ❑ Clamps
- ❑ Chisel (optional)
- ❑ Rotary power tool (optional)

Cutting the Pieces

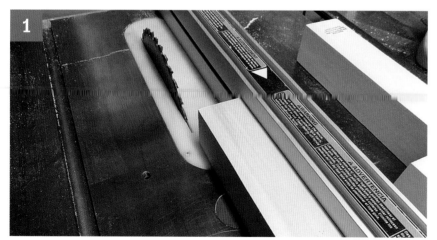

1. Use a table saw to cut the blanks to size. You can also cut them with your choice of saw, and use a disc sander or belt sander to sand the blanks to the exact dimensions. Cover the blanks with blue painter's tape. Fold the patterns on the dotted lines, apply adhesive to the backs of the patterns, align the folds with the corners of the blanks, and press the patterns into place.

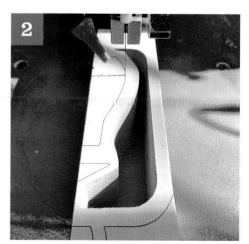

2. Drill ⅛" (3mm) blade-entry holes in both sides for the inside cuts. Make the interior cuts on the first side with a #9 blade. Be careful because the saw arm or the blade holder may pinch your fingers against the wood when you are cutting thick wood.

PATTERN LOCATED ON PAGE 81

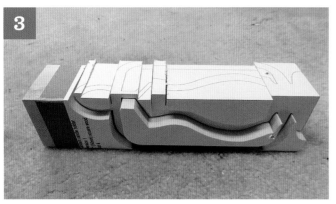

3. Cut the perimeter lines on one side and replace the waste pieces. Use small pieces of clear tape to hold the waste in place while you wrap the blank with clear packaging tape to secure the pieces.

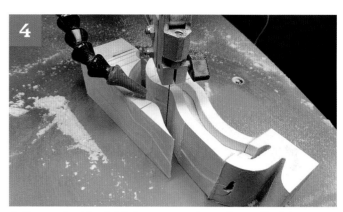

4. Rotate the blank 90 degrees, and cut along all of the pattern lines. Carefully separate the piece from the waste. Remove the pattern and tape, and hand-sand away any visible irregularities. Remove the sanding dust with a stiff-bristled paintbrush. Use the process explained in the previous steps to cut the other three quarters of the lantern.

Assembling the Lantern

5. Glue and clamp two sets of quarters together to create two halves. Remove any glue squeeze-out with a damp rag. Cover the areas that will be glued together with tape, and apply finish to the inside of the lantern. I use spray lacquer.

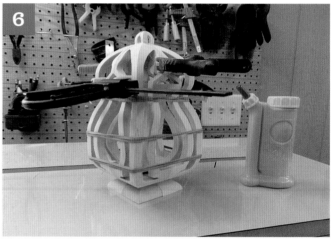

6. Glue together the two halves and clamp them in place. Rubber bands work well to hold the pieces together while the glue dries.

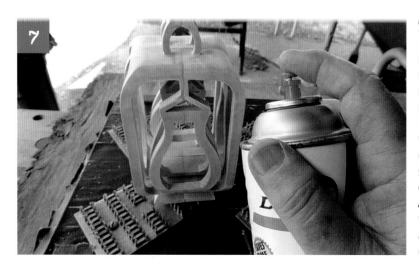

7. Use a chisel, rotary-power carver, or sandpaper to smooth the profile of the lantern as needed, especially along the glue joints. Hand-sand the lanterns with progressively finer grits of sandpaper to get a smooth finish. Apply several coats of clear spray lacquer. Allow the lacquer to dry thoroughly between coats, and sand lightly with 500-grit sandpaper.

Garden Lanterns

Photocopy at 100%

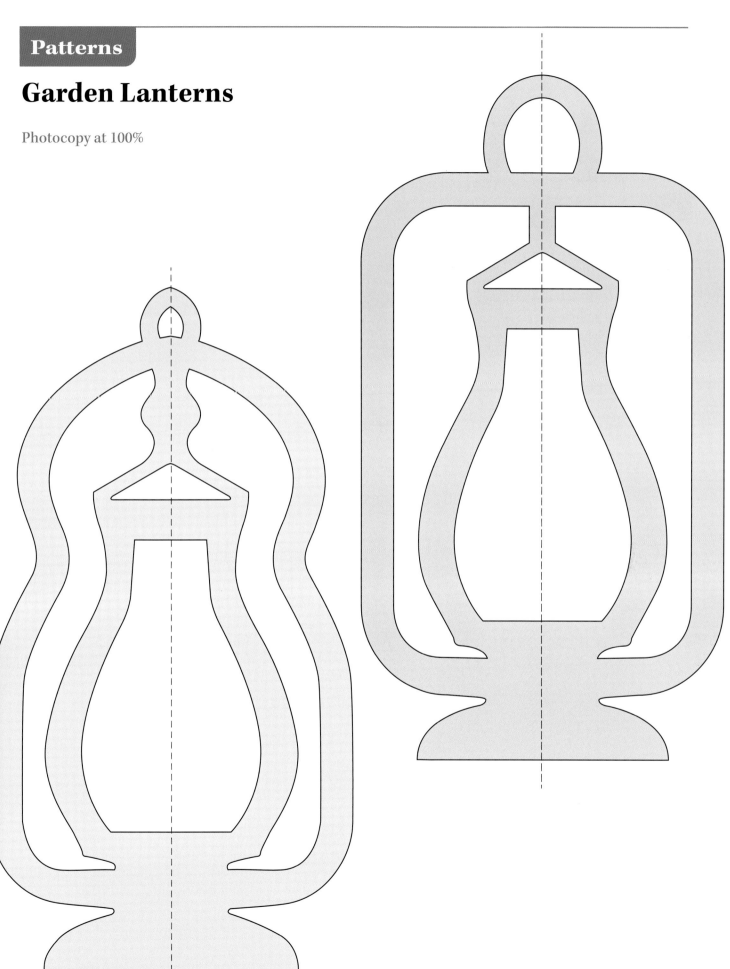

Opposing Forces Bookends

Easy compound figures add some fun to your book collection

BY FRED AND JULIE BYRNE

CUT BY DALE HELGERSON

These bookends make a great gift and are a whimsical addition to any library or desk. The 3D figures look impressive, but are easy to make. Individual segments are created using compound-cutting techniques, which are then glued together to form the figure.

Getting Started

1. Cut the outline of the patterns. Fold the patterns along the dotted line. Cut the blanks to size. Wrap clear packaging tape around the blanks to lubricate the blade.

MATERIALS

For the Pushing Forward Man

- ❏ Beech wood blank: ¾" (1.9cm) thick x 1½" x 3⁵/₁₆" (38 x 8.4cm) (leg)
- ❏ Beech wood blank: ¾" (1.9cm) thick x 1³/₁₆" x 2¹³/₁₆" (30 x 7.1cm) (leg)
- ❏ 2 beech wood blanks: ¾" (1.9cm) thick x 1" x 1½" (25 x 38mm) (arms)
- ❏ Beech wood blank: ¾" (1.9cm) thick x ⅞" x 1³/₃₂" (22 x 2.8cm) (head)
- ❏ 2 beech wood blanks: ¾" (1.9cm) thick x ⅞" x 1⅝" (22 x 4.1cm) (torso)

For the Pushing Back Man

- ❏ 2 beech wood blanks: ¾" (1.9cm) thick x ¾" x 2¹¹/₁₆" (19 x 6.8cm) (arms)
- ❏ Beech wood blank: ¾" (1.9cm) thick x 1½" x 3¹⁵/₁₆" (38 x 8.4cm) (leg)
- ❏ Beech wood blank: ¾" (1.9cm) thick x 1³/₈" x 3¹³/₁₆" (35 x 9.7cm) (leg)
- ❏ 2 beech wood blanks: ¾" (1.9cm) thick x ⅞" x 1¹⁵/₁₆" (22 x 33mm) (torso)
- ❏ Beech wood blank: ¾" (1.9cm) thick x 1" x 1¹⁵/₁₆" beech (25 x 33mm) (head)

For the Bookend Bases

- ❏ 2 walnut wood blanks: ¾" (1.9cmm) thick x 4" x 6½" (10.2 x 16.5cm) (uprights)
- ❏ 2 walnut wood blanks: ¾" (1.9cmm) thick x 3½" x 4" (8.m x 16.5cm) (bases)

- ❏ 4 walnut plugs: ³/₈" (1mm) diameter
- ❏ PVA wood glue
- ❏ Cyanoacrylate (CA) glue
- ❏ Glue stick or spray adhesive
- ❏ Clear packaging tape
- ❏ Cling wrap
- ❏ Sandpaper, assorted grits up to 320
- ❏ Acrylic wood sealer
- ❏ Clear liquid polish
- ❏ Tack cloth
- ❏ Soft lint-free cloth
- ❏ 4 (#8) wood screws 1½" (38mm) long

TOOLS

- ❏ Scroll saw with blades: #7 skip-tooth
- ❏ Saw blade lubricant (optional)
- ❏ Drill press with bit: ¹/₈" (3mm) diameter with countersink collar
- ❏ Paintbrushes
- ❏ Sanding block
- ❏ Screwdriver

PATTERN LOCATED ON PAGE 135

Opposing Forces Bookends **83**

Cutting

2. Use spray adhesive or a glue stick on the back of the paper pattern. Align the fold of the pattern with the corner of the blank, and press the pattern in place.

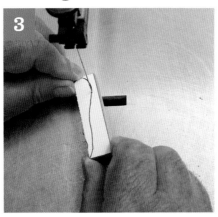

3. Use a #7 skip-tooth blade. Make sure the blade is square to the saw table. Complete the cut of the first profile. Do not discard the waste.

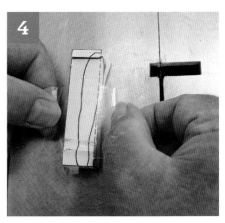

4. Hold the piece in place inside the waste, and tape the blank together with clear packaging tape. Complete the cut, of the second profile, on the other side of the blank.

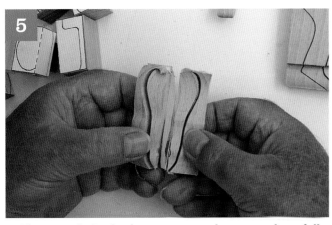

5. After completing both cuts, remove the tape and carefully remove the waste pieces. The 3D piece will emerge from the center.

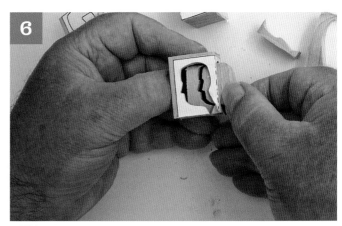

6. Use the same technique to cut the other parts. Carefully remove the waste to reveal the 3D piece in the center of each blank.

Finishing and Assembling

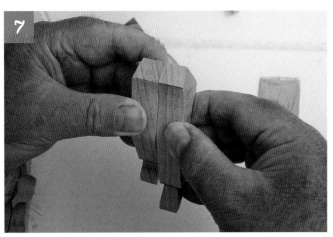

7. Check to make sure the legs and torso fit together properly. Then, make sure the head and arms fit onto the torso properly.

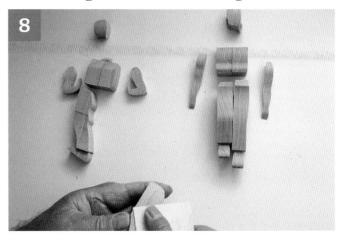

8. Start sanding with 180-grit sandpaper. Then, sand the pieces again with 240-grit sandpaper. Wipe the pieces with a tack cloth to remove the dust.

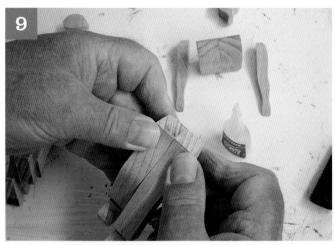

9. Tape cling wrap to the workbench to prevent the figures from sticking to the bench. Align the tops of the legs, and glue them together using cyanoacrylate (CA) glue.

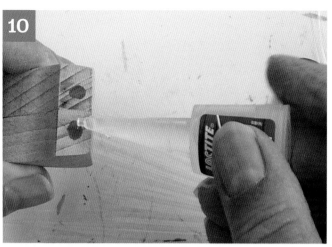

10. Work on one figure at a time. Attach the torso to the legs. Attach the arms and head to the torso. Position the figure against a vertical wall to help with placement.

11. Assemble the base. Drill and countersink two ⅛" pilot holes through the upright into each base. Apply wood glue to the edge of each base and attach the pieces with 1 ½" (38mm) long wood screws. Glue ⅜" (10mm) plugs in place over the screw heads. Sand the bases with 240-grit sandpaper and remove the dust with a tack cloth.

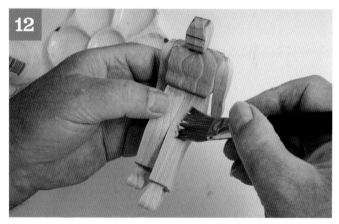

12. Use a paintbrush to apply an acrylic sanding sealer to all of the pieces, including the figures. You do not need to seal the parts of the figures that will be glued to the bookends. Remove the excess sealer with a lint-free cloth and a dry brush. Allow the sealer to dry. Rub down the wood with 320-grit sandpaper. Remove the dust with a tack cloth.

13. Use an old paintbrush to apply wood glue to the area where each figure attaches to the base and uprights. Center each figure on the appropriate bookend and wipe away any excess glue. Allow the glue to dry completely.

14. Apply a liquid polish to make the wooden bookends feel silky smooth. Brush the liquid polish onto the wood. When the polish is dry, buff it to a nice sheen with a soft cloth or brush.

Magnetic Tic-Tac-Toe Game

Clever compound-cut pieces stay put for fun on the run

BY SUE MEY

Tic-tac-toe is one of the first games children learn. This version uses magnets and metal. For straight blade-entry holes and neat inside cuts, it is crucial that the blocks have perfectly straight edges at a 90-degree angle to each other. I use a combination of hardwood and stained MDF for my tic-tac-toe board, but various materials will work, including plywood. For a full overlay pattern, join four copies of the overlay pattern together. For the game pieces, make five copies of each pattern.

MATERIALS

For the Game Board

- ❑ Wood blank: 2" (5.1cm) thick x10¾" (27.3cm) square (game board base)
- ❑ Plywood or MDF wood blank: ⅛" (3mm) thick x 10¾" (27.3cm) square (overlay)
- ❑ Magnetic metal sheet, 10¾" (27.3cm) square
- ❑ Scrap plywood: ⅛" to ¼" (3 to 6mm) thick x 10¾" (27.3cm) square (to cut metal on)

For the Game Pieces

- ❑ 10 wood blanks: 1½" (3.8cm) thick x 1½" x 2 ½" (3.8cm x 4.4cm)
- ❑ Masking tape
- ❑ Clear packaging tape
- ❑ Magnetic sheeting
- ❑ Spray adhesive or glue stick
- ❑ Sandpaper, assorted grits up to 600
- ❑ Deep-penetrating furniture wax liquid or Danish oil
- ❑ Dark brown spray paint
- ❑ Gold spray paint
- ❑ Clear spray varnish

- ❑ Walnut wood stain
- ❑ Lint-free cloth
- ❑ Wood glue
- ❑ Fine-tipped gold paint pen
- ❑ Black permanent marker
- ❑ Pencil

TOOLS

- ❑ Scroll saw with blades: #2, #7, & #12 skip-tooth, #2 steel-cutting or blades of choice
- ❑ Drill press with bit ¼" (9mm) diameter
- ❑ Small-size artist's brushes
- ❑ Medium-size artist's brushes
- ❑ Disc sander
- ❑ Scraper blade
- ❑ Square
- ❑ Clamps
- ❑ Scissors
- ❑ Needle files
- ❑ Vacuum
- ❑ Ruler

Cutting the Parts

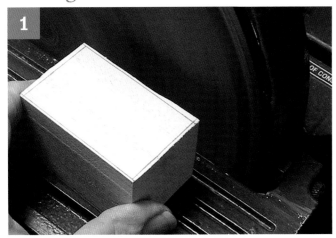

1. Cut the thick game pieces and game board base with a #12 blade. Switch to a #2 blade for the overlay. Square up the cuts with a disc sander. Cover the overlay piece with masking tape, and use spray adhesive to attach the patterns to the appropriate blanks.

2. Use a ⅛" (3mm) drill bit to drill the entry holes. For best results, use a drill press; the holes need to be straight through the blank. Remove the rough edges created by the drilling process with sandpaper or a scraper blade.

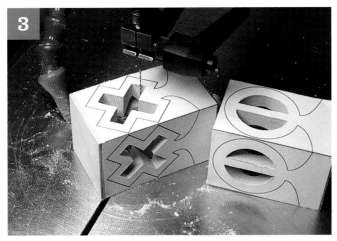

3. Use a #2 blade to cut the overlay pattern. Remove the small squares and the large inside square. Switch to a #7 blade to make the inside cuts on both sides of the game pieces and remove the waste.

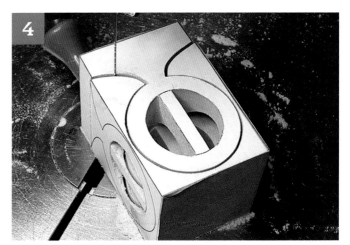

4. Make a single uninterrupted cut. Hold the piece in place while you vacuum away the dust. Wrap clear packaging tape around the block to hold the cut piece in place. Turn the blank and cut along the second line. Remove the waste pieces.

5. Make sure the metal backing is attracted to a magnet. Use a square, a ruler, and a black permanent marker to draw the dimensions of the board onto the metal sheet. Place the metal on top of a piece of scrap plywood, wrap the stack with clear packing tape, and cut along the lines with a #2 steel blade. File the cut edges to remove any rough edges.

6. Attach the overlay to the game board base with double-sided tape, and sand up to the pattern lines with a disc sander. Remove the tape and patterns, and sand the surfaces, including the game pieces, with 320-grit sandpaper. Switch to 500-grit sandpaper and sand the pieces again. Clean up the frets with needle files. Remove all the sanding dust.

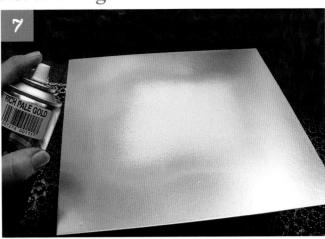

7. Use a medium-sized artist's brush to apply walnut wood stain to the overlay. Allow it to dry. Apply deep-penetrating furniture wax liquid or Danish oil to the game pieces and the game board base with a medium-sized artist's brush. Place the items in the sun to dry, and wipe all the surfaces with a dry lint-free cloth.

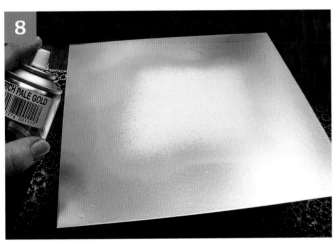

8. Apply gold spray paint to the outer edges of the metal sheet. Allow it to dry thoroughly. Using the overlay as a guide, cover the edges of the metal with 2" (5.1cm)-wide masking tape. Apply several coats of dark brown spray paint to the center, allowing the paint to dry thoroughly between coats. Carefully remove the masking tape after the brown paint is dry.

9. Apply wood glue to the game board base, position the metal on top, clamp it in place, and allow the glue to dry. With the overlay in place, use a ruler and sharp pencil to mark the positions of the lines on the metal. Remove the overlay and carefully draw the lines using a gold paint pen and a square. Allow the paint lines to dry before gluing and clamping the overlay to the game board base.

10. To finish the pieces, apply several thin coats of clear spray varnish to the board and the game pieces. Allow the varnish to dry thoroughly, and sand the game pieces with 600-grit sandpaper between coats. Cut squares of self-adhesive magnetic sheeting and attach them to the bottom of the game pieces. Make sure the magnetic sheeting is strong enough to secure the pieces; not all magnets are strong enough to secure the pieces.

Hardwood Chess Set

A nested design provides a new twist on the classic strategy game

BY CLAYTON MEYERS

This chess set, which will take you some time to complete, makes an excellent conversation piece and will turn heads when on display. The pieces are made by compound cutting, the technique used throughout this book that involves cutting on two sides of the blank to create a 3D piece. To review, after you cut one side, you tape the scrap back onto the blank, rotate it 90 degrees, and make the second set of cuts. Remove the scrap and the 3D piece is revealed. Choose maple, walnut, cherry, purpleheart, or zebrawood.

MATERIALS

- ❏ 32 maple, walnut, or cherry wood blanks: 1½" (3.8cm) square x 3½" to 6⅝" (8.9 to 16.8cm) long
- ❏ Spray adhesive
- ❏ Clear packaging tape
- ❏ Sandpaper, 220-grit
- ❏ Finish, such as high-gloss polyurethane
- ❏ Fishing line

TOOLS

- ❏ Table saw or miter saw
- ❏ Scroll saw with blades:#1, #2/0, #3, #5 skip-tooth
- ❏ Rotary tool or coping saw (optional)
- ❏ Drill press with bits: assorted small
- ❏ Jeweler's files
- ❏ Small paintbrush
- ❏ Small square
- ❏ Utility knife

Squaring Your Blade

Use a small square to make sure your blade is square from side to side. Then, secure the top of the blade as far back in the upper blade clamp as possible. Hold the blade against a small square as you clamp the bottom of the blade. Run your saw on the slowest speed possible, and let the blade scrape against the edge of a piece of wood that you know is 100 percent square. Just let the tips of the blade teeth barely scratch the wood. If you notice it is scratching more at the top or bottom, adjust the blade accordingly. Adjust the blade at the bottom clamp only. This way, when you release the top of the blade to move from inside cut to inside cut, you can push the blade all the way to the back of the clamp and know you are still square.

PATTERN LOCATED ON PAGES 137–138

Hardwood Chess Set **91**

Getting Started

1. Measure each pattern and cut each blank to length. Next, make sure your blade is exactly square with the table. If the blade is not square to the table, you will end up overcutting in some areas and undercutting in others. This leads to ugly tool marks on your final product. Additionally, plan to go through two to three blades per piece. Change blades often; dull blades burn the wood and cut more slowly.

Preparing to Cut

2. Cut the patterns. Make a scoring cut along the fold line with a knife; this helps you get a sharp fold. Apply spray adhesive to the back. Align the fold with the corner of the blank and press the pattern into place. Use a miter saw or table saw to trim the blank precisely at the bottom of the feet and remove some of the excess from the top.

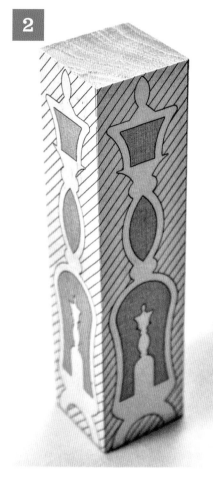

3. Using a drill press, drill the blade-entry holes on both sides. Use a bit just large enough to fit your scroll saw blade through, and make sure the hole is perfectly square to the top of the blank. Position the holes near the corners, so you don't need to cut sharp corners. Lightly sand the sides opposite to the patterns to remove any burrs from the drilling process. Wrap all four sides of the blank with clear packaging tape to secure the pattern and to help prevent burning.

Cutting the Pieces

4. Make the inside cuts. I use a #5 skip-tooth blade to remove the excess wood. This blade cuts fast without being hard to control or leaving excessive blade marks. Rotate the blank 90 degrees, and repeat the process on the other side. Switch to a #1 skip-tooth blade to cut the more delicate details.

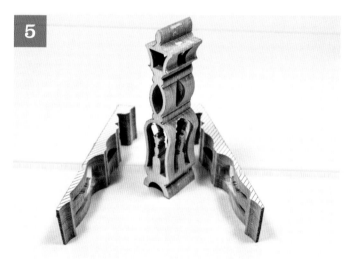

5. Switch back to the first side. Cut around the perimeter using a #3 skip-tooth blade. While this blade cuts slowly, you must make this cut accurately on the first pass. Start at the bottom of the piece and keep the blade directly on the line. At sharp corners, cut all the way into the corner, back out slightly, and make the turn. Be gentle with the scrap; you'll tape it back in place to cut the second side. Cut out at the top. Repeat for the other half of the first side. Go back and clean up any corners.

6. Remove all sawdust and chips from the piece and scrap.
Use clear packaging tape to secure the scrap back to the chess piece. Rotate the blank 90 degrees, and cut along the perimeter of the other side. Remove the piece from the scrap. Note the "shadows" of the inside figure on all four sides of the piece. They'll be removed later.

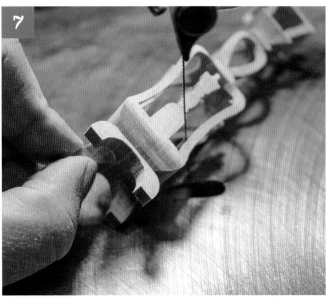

7. Remove the shadows from all four sides. While it's possible to use a rotary tool or a coping saw, if you are careful, you can cut it away with a scroll saw. Use a #2/0 blade and insert it into the inside cut. Set your saw to the slowest possible speed; any slip or blade chatter will crack and ruin the chess piece. Hold the piece at an angle, and carefully cut the shadow on two sides at a time. Do not cut into the frame or the inner piece.

Finishing the Pieces

8. Remove any small burs. Use 220-grit sandpaper or jeweler's files. Apply two coats of high-gloss polyurethane or your finish of choice. I string the pieces on fishing line and dip them directly into the can of finish. Lift them out and use a small paintbrush to remove the excess.

Sign of a Dull Blade

Don't be afraid to get a new blade. When cutting thick hardwood, it may not always be clear when your blade is dull. Look for discolored sawdust. If the dust is darker than the wood itself, change blades. You will find it easier to cut.

Eiffel Tower Desk Sitter

Give your space Parisian flair with this chic compound-cut decoration

BY SUE MEY

CUT BY JON DECK

You will use four identical patterns to make this project. Cut the four blanks to size using a table saw. (You can also cut them with your saw of choice and use a disc sander or belt sander to sand the blanks to the exact dimensions.) The blanks must be precisely cut and/or sanded to size before applying the patterns. Cover the blanks with masking tape or blue painter's tape. Then, fold the patterns on the center lines, apply spray adhesive to the backs, align the folds with the corners of the blanks, and press the patterns into place.

MATERIALS

- ❏ 4 basswood, butternut, or cedar wood blanks: 1⁷⁄₈" (4.8cm) square x 7" (17.8cm) long
- ❏ Masking or blue painter's tape
- ❏ Clear packaging tape
- ❏ Spray adhesive
- ❏ Sandpaper, assorted grits
- ❏ Wood glue
- ❏ Finish, such as clear spray varnish or white milk paint

TOOLS

- ❏ Table saw
- ❏ Disc sander or stationary 4" belt sander (optional)
- ❏ Scroll saw with blades: #9 skip reverse
- ❏ Drill press with bit: 1⁄₈" (3mm) diameter
- ❏ Air compressor or ice pick (optional)
- ❏ Stiff-bristled paintbrush
- ❏ Clamps (or large rubber bands)
- ❏ Vacuum

1. Drill ⅛" (3mm) blade-entry holes in both sides for the frets. Using a #9 scroll saw blade, cut the frets on one side, and then cut the perimeter. Saw all the way through the wood, but stop just before cutting the paper free, leaving the pattern intact. This will make it easier to cut the other side. Vacuum away the dust, and tape the waste pieces back in place with clear packaging tape.

2. Rotate the blank 90 degrees and cut the second side. Carefully remove the completed section from the waste and peel off any remaining patterns or tape. After making the final cuts, save the outer waste pieces. An ice pick or air compressor is handy to remove small waste pieces. You can also blow out the pieces using an air compressor.

3. Carefully match up the outer waste pieces and the inner (non-waste) pieces. This will give you square sides to clamp to. Glue and clamp together two pieces (each representing a quarter of the completed project). Note: Make sure the pieces line up nicely. Use great care not to get any glue on the outside of the project; otherwise, you will glue the waste pieces back onto the cut pieces. Then, assemble the other half using the same technique. Glue and clamp the two halves together. Once the glue has dried, remove the clamps.

4. Hand-sand the outside surfaces of the project to remove irregularities. Remove all sanding dust with a stiff-bristled paintbrush. Finish as desired; I used several thin coats of clear spray varnish on one version and white milk paint on the other.

PATTERN LOCATED ON PAGE 132

Eiffel Tower Desk Sitter **95**

Compound Candleholders

Solid wood stands support small candles

BY SUE MEY

CUT BY LELDON MAXCY

These candleholders are particularly attractive if they are cut from blanks made of laminated hardwood species. Use the stands to display battery-operated tea lights, votives, or small pillar candles, adding glass holders as needed.

MATERIALS

- ❏ 2 wood blanks: 2" (5.1cm) thick x 2" x 6¼" (5.1 x 15.9cm)
- ❏ Masking tape
- ❏ Clear packaging tape
- ❏ Spray adhesive or glue stick
- ❏ Sandpaper, 320 and 600-grit
- ❏ Clear spray varnish
- ❏ Battery-operated tea light candles or small votive candles in glass holders
- ❏ Deep-penetrating furniture wax liquid or Danish oil (optional)
- ❏ Lint-free cloth

TOOLS

- ❏ Scroll saw with blades: #7, #9, or #12 skip-tooth
- ❏ Drill press with bit: ⅛" (3mm) diameter
- ❏ Needle files
- ❏ Stiff-bristled paintbrush
- ❏ Medium-size artist's paintbrush
- ❏ Vacuum

Cutting and Finishing

1. Fold the patterns along the dotted lines. Cover the blanks with masking tape. Use spray adhesive or a glue stick to attach the patterns to the blanks.

2. Drill ⅛" (3mm) blade-entry holes. Using a #7 or #9 blade for softer wood or a #12 blade for hardwood, make the inside cuts on both sides of the project.

3. To cut the perimeter, make a single uninterrupted cut on each side. Vacuum away the dust. Wrap clear packaging tape around the block to hold the cut pieces in place. Rotate the blank 90 degrees, and cut along the pattern lines. Remove the waste pieces.

4. Clean the frets with needle files or sandpaper as needed. Sand the pieces with 320-grit sandpaper. Remove all sanding dust using a stiff-bristled paintbrush.

5. Apply a finish to the pieces (optional). Use a medium-sized artist's brush to apply deep-penetrating furniture wax or Danish oil to the ornaments. Wipe all surfaces with a dry, lint-free cloth to remove any residue, and place them in the sun to dry.

6. Apply several thin coats of clear spray varnish to the pieces, sanding with 600-grit sandpaper between coats. Allow the varnish to dry thoroughly.

PATTERN
LOCATED ON
PAGE 139

Easy Vases

Scroll a sturdy vessel for your favorite flower

BY SUE MEY

CUT BY JOE PASCUCCI

Display your fresh-cut flowers in a handsome vase you've made yourself. The designs are relatively simple to cut and can be completed in an afternoon; the hollow center houses a glass tube insert for water. Finish them as desired; you can use acrylics, stains, and dyes, or leave them natural.

MATERIALS

- ❏ 2 pine, spalted maple, aromatic cedar, or walnut wood blanks: 2" (5.1cm) square x 8" (20.3cm) long
- ❏ Masking tape or blue painter's tape
- ❏ Clear packaging tape
- ❏ Spray adhesive or glue stick
- ❏ Sandpaper, assorted grits up to 320
- ❏ Finish, such as clear satin spray varnish
- ❏ Glass vase tube, ¾" (19mm) diameter
- ❏ Acrylic paints, dyes, or stains (optional)

TOOLS

- ❏ Scroll saw with blades: #5, #7, or #9 reverse-tooth
- ❏ Drill press with bit: Forstner ¾" (19mm) diameter
- ❏ Vacuum
- ❏ Square
- ❏ Stiff-bristled paintbrush
- ❏ Holding jig or vise

Getting Started

1. Cut the pattern blank to size, making sure that the sides are flat and at a 90-degree angle to each other. Cover two adjacent faces of the blank with masking or blue painter's tape. Then, use spray adhesive or a glue stick to attach the pattern to the surface of the tape, lining the centerline of the pattern up with the corner of the blank.

2. Hollow out the center of the blank. If you wish to use a smaller glass insert, adjust the drill bit size accordingly. Before drilling, check to make sure the drill press table and bit are aligned at 90 degrees. Secure the blank in a holding jig or vise, and then drill to a depth of 3½" (8.9cm) with a ¾" (19mm) Forstner bit. To keep the bit from overheating, drill in increments of ½" (1.3cm) or less. After each increment, back out the bit completely and vacuum up all wood shavings.

Cutting and Finishing

3. Select a blade size appropriate for the thickness and hardness of the wood being used. I use a #5 or #7 blade for softer wood like pine, but for something harder, such as maple or walnut, consider a #9. Use a scroll saw to make the cuts on one side of the blank. Hold the waste pieces in place with clear packaging tape, rotate the blank 90 degrees, and then make the cuts on the second side. Remove the waste wood.

4. Sand all the surfaces by hand, and remove sanding dust with a stiff-bristled paintbrush. Apply several coats of clear spray varnish or a finish of choice. Add the glass insert and display as desired.

PATTERN LOCATED ON PAGES 140–141

Fretwork Vase

This elegant project is better than the sum of its parts

BY SUE MEY

CUT BY DENNIS KNAPPEN

Most scroll saws struggle to cut wood thicker than 2" (5.1cm), but if you cut four pieces and glue them together, you can make this nearly 4" (10.2cm)-diameter vase. These patterns are sized for 1⅞" (4.8cm)-thick wood; if your saw cannot cut wood this thick, reduce the patterns slightly to fit the thickest wood you can cut. Add the glass insert. Fill the finished product with cut flowers and herbs, or wrap it up for a friend's housewarming as a stylish and meaningful gift.

MATERIALS

- ❑ 4 basswood, jelutong, butternut, or cedar wood blanks: 1⅞" (4.8cm) square x 7¼" (18.4cm) long
- ❑ Spray adhesive
- ❑ Wood glue
- ❑ Finish, such as clear spray lacquer
- ❑ Glass bud vase, ¾" (19mm) diameter

TOOLS

- ❑ Scroll saw with blades: #9 skip-tooth
- ❑ Drill press with bits: ⅛" (3mm) diameter twist, ¾" (19mm) diameter Forstner or extra-long spade
- ❑ Drill bit extension
- ❑ Vacuum
- ❑ Clamps

Cutting and Finishing

1. Make four copies of the pattern. Fold each pattern on the dotted line. Apply spray adhesive to the back of each, align the fold with the corner of the blank, and press it into place. Drill all the blade-entry holes.

2. Cut the frets on one face. Rotate the blank 90 degrees and cut the other frets.

3. Cut the perimeter of one side. Remove the dust with a vacuum and tape the cut pieces back in place. Rotate the blank 90 degrees. Cut the perimeter of the other side. Remove the pieces from the waste wood. Repeat the above steps for the other three pieces.

4. Glue and clamp together two pieces to create half the vase. Repeat with the other two pieces. Allow the glue to dry.

5. Glue and clamp the two halves together. Hand-sand the outside surfaces to remove any irregularities.

6. Drill the hole for the bud vase. Use a ¾" (19mm) Forstner or spade bit. Drill the hole deep enough to accommodate the bud vase, usually at least 6" (15.2cm) deep. You might need to use an extra-long drill bit or drill bit extension.

7. Apply several coats of clear spray lacquer to the assembled vase. Allow the finish to dry thoroughly between coats. Insert the glass bud vase and add your flowers!

PATTERN LOCATED ON PAGE 133

Musical Instruments

Photocopy at 100%

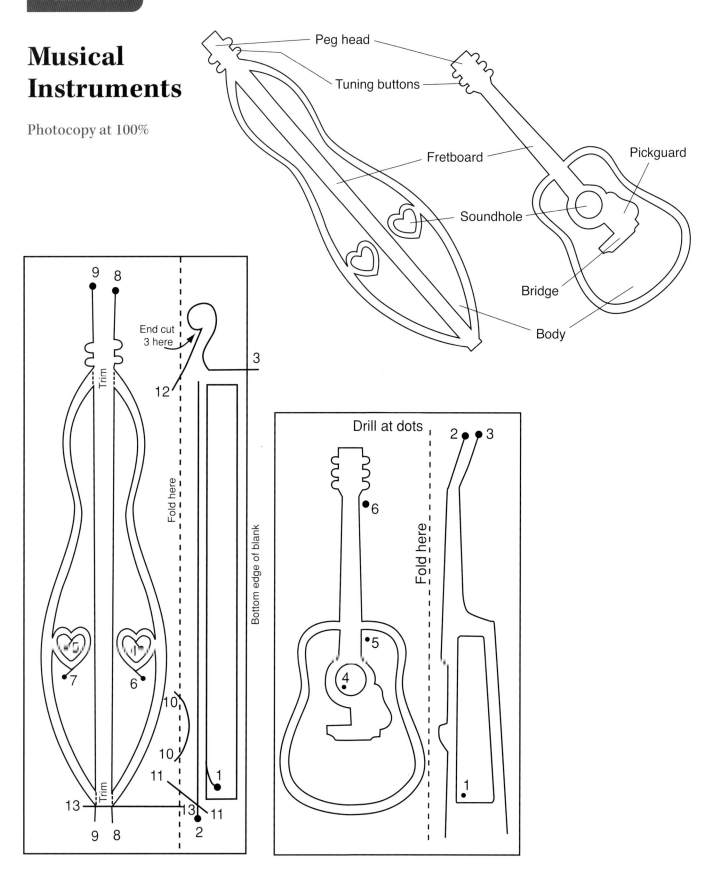

Peg head

Tuning buttons

Fretboard

Pickguard

Soundhole

Bridge

Body

End cut 3 here

Trim

Fold here

Bottom edge of blank

Trim

Drill at dots

Fold here

Feathers and Leaves

Photocopy at 100%

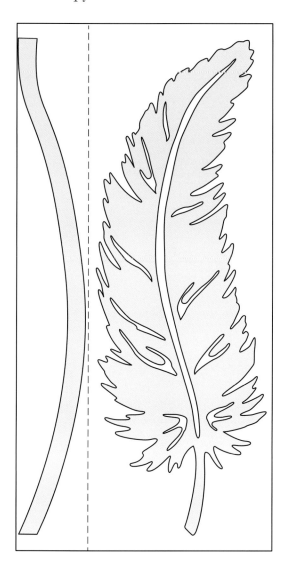

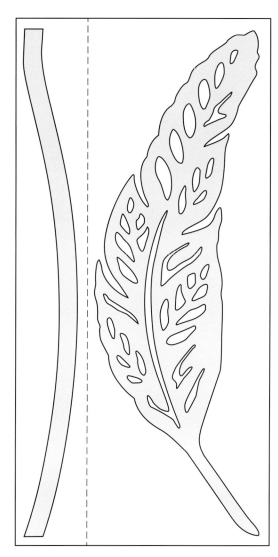

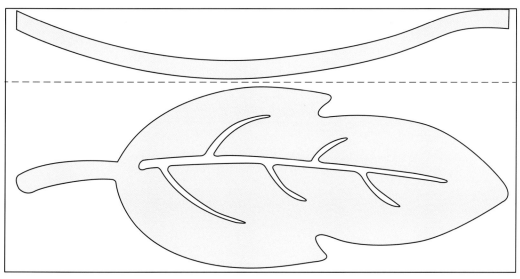

Feathers and Leaves

Photocopy at 100%

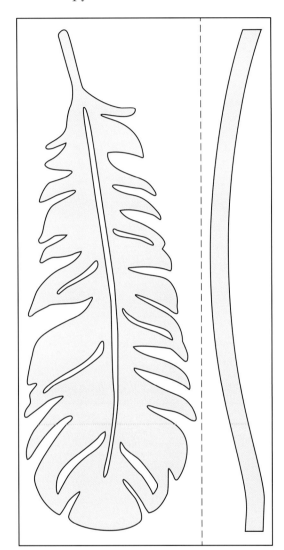
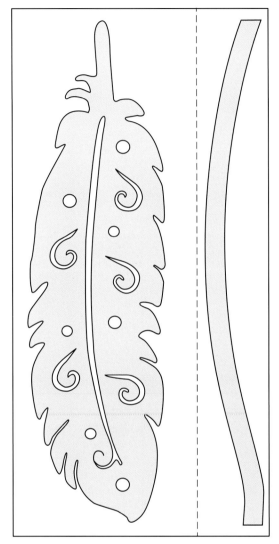

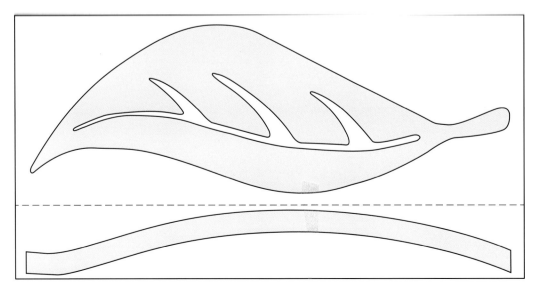

Snowflake Ornaments

Enlarge by 125%

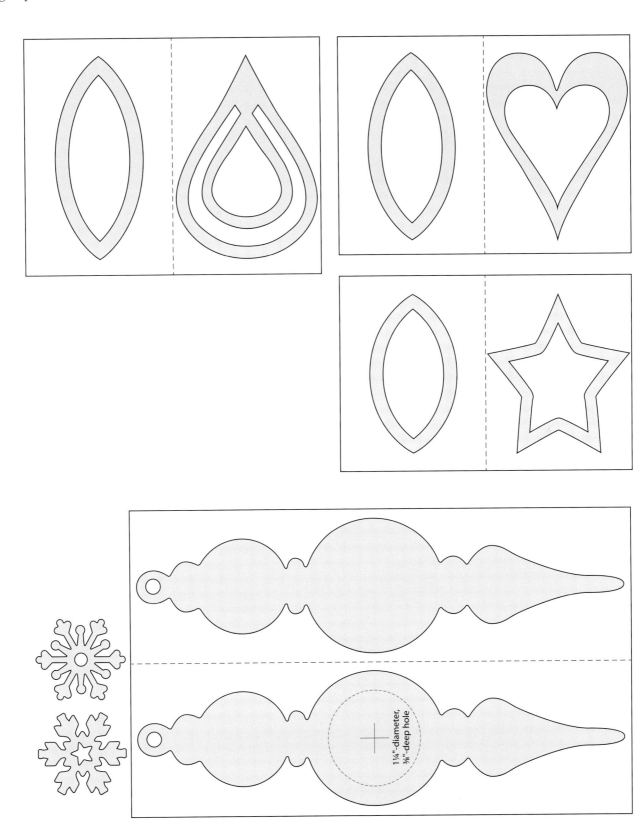

1¼"-diameter, ⅜" deep hole

Snowflake Ornaments

Enlarge by 125%

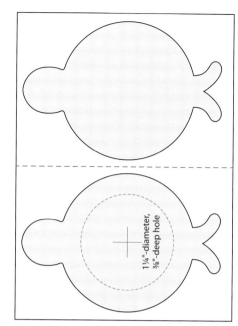

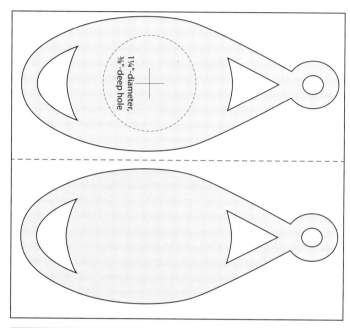

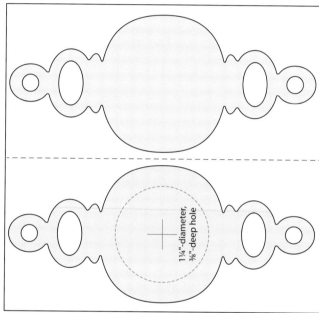

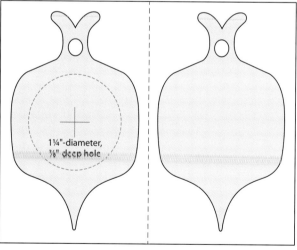

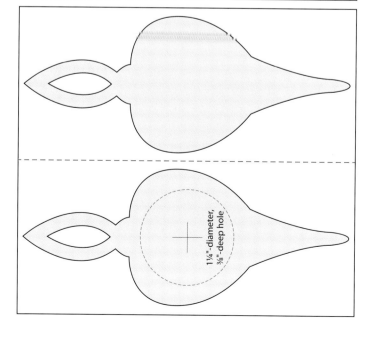

3D Christmas Ornament

Photocopy at 100%

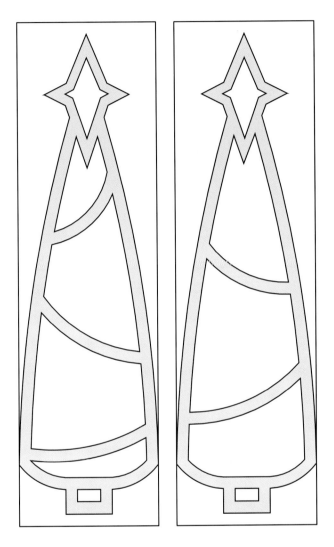

Present Ornament

Photocopy at 100%

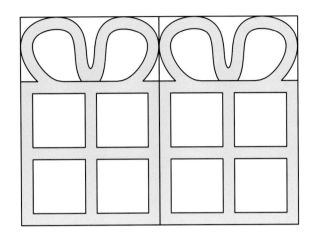

Finial Ornaments

Photocopy at 100%

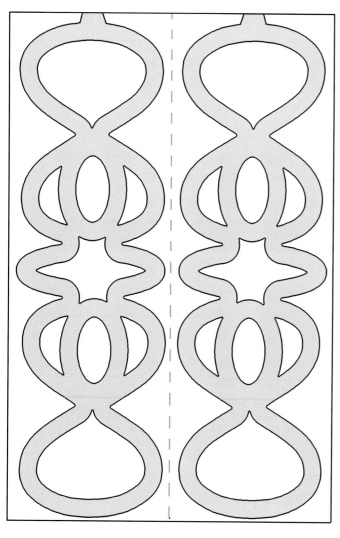

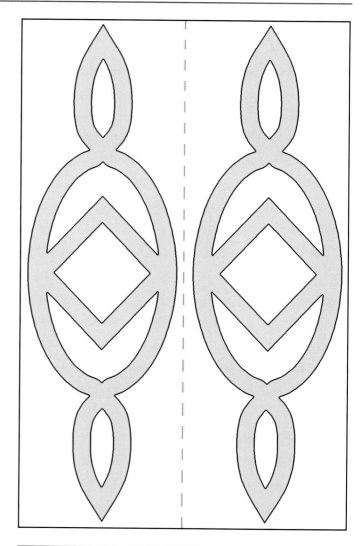

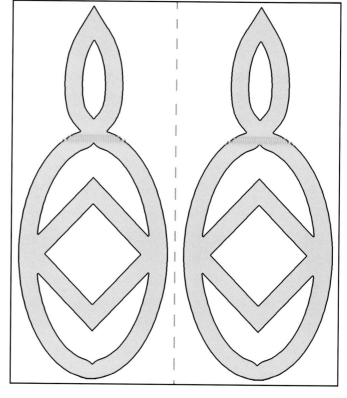

Finial Ornaments

Photocopy at 100%

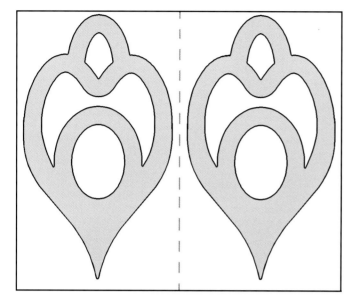

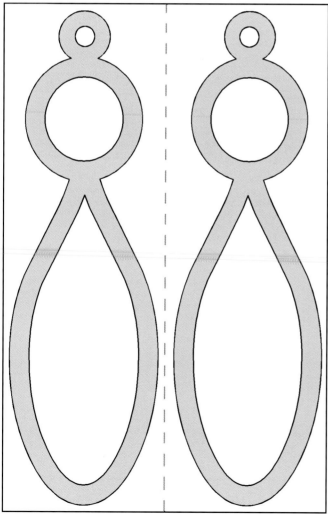

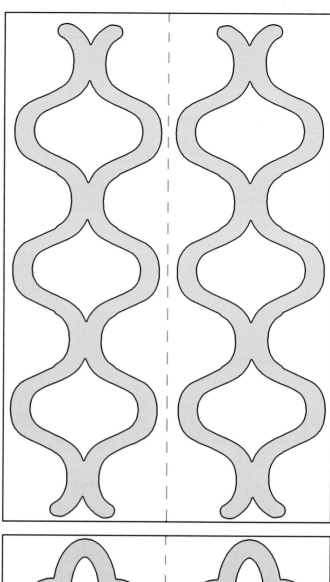

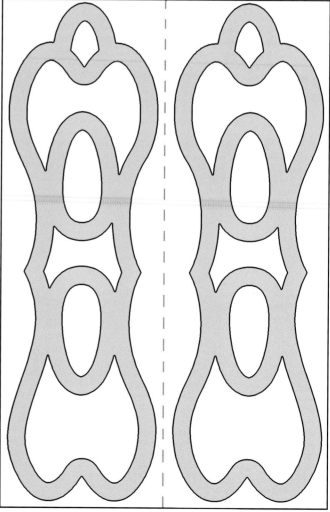

Songbird in a Birdcage

Photocopy at 100%

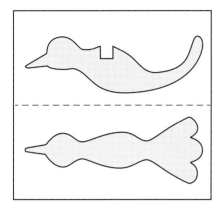

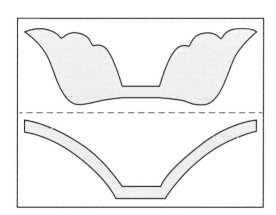

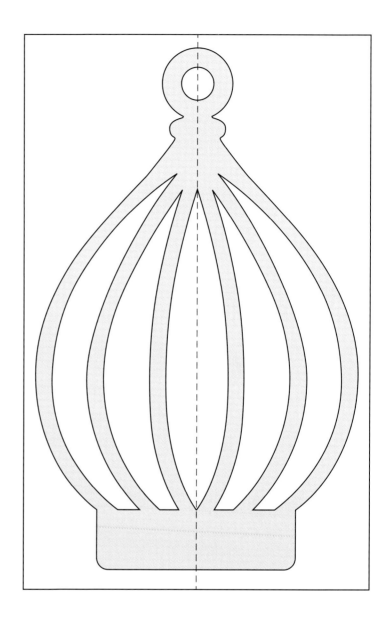

Ornament Earrings

Photocopy at 100%

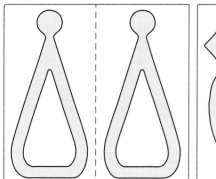

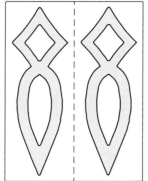

Birds of a Feather

Photocopy at 100%

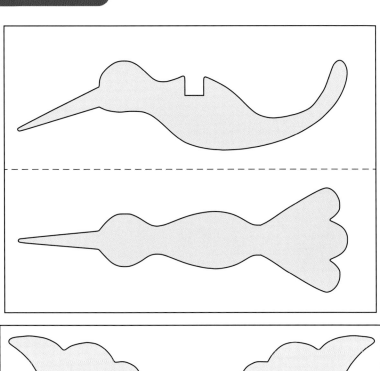

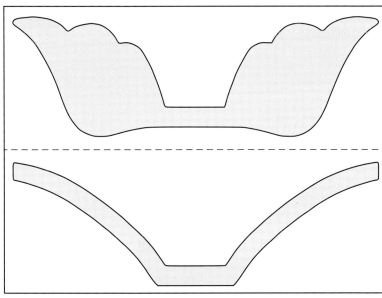

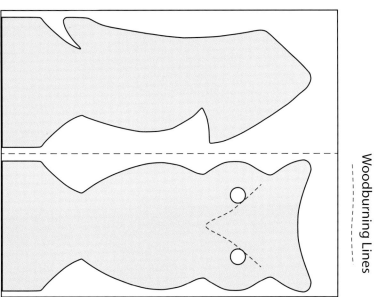

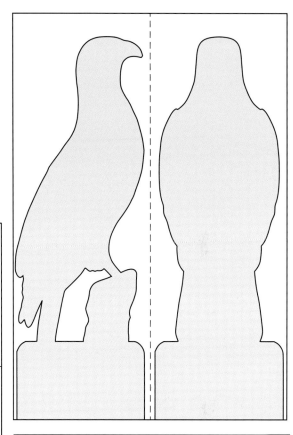

Woodburning Lines
– – – – –

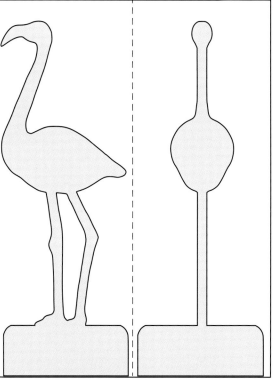

Floral Arrangement

Photocopy at 100%

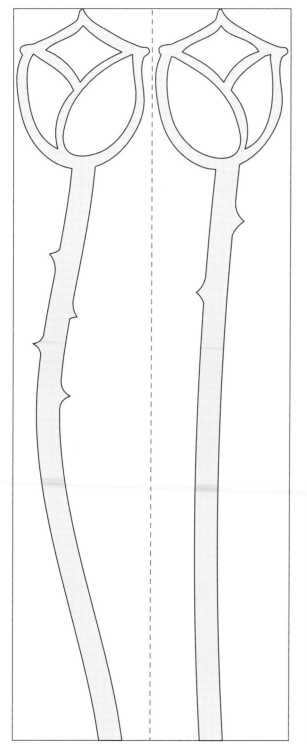

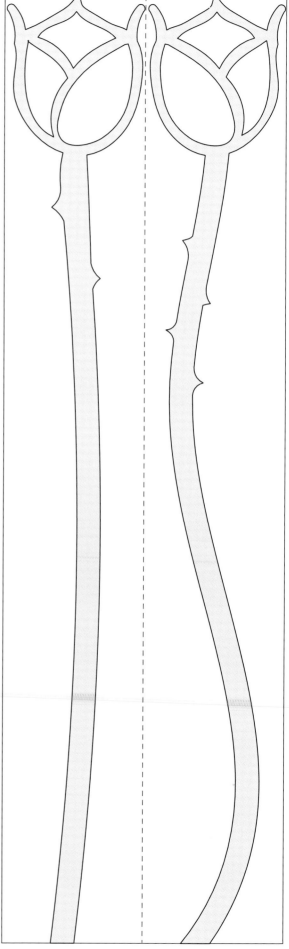

Floral Arrangement

Photocopy at 100%

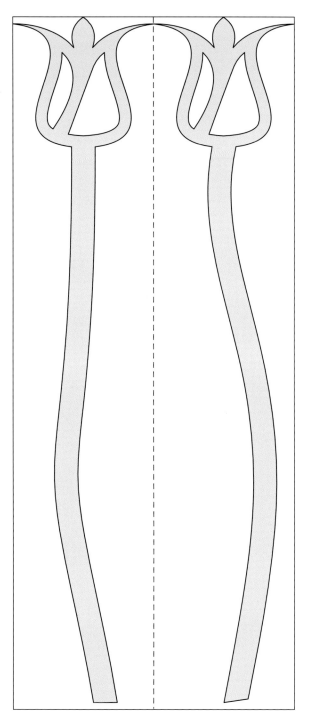

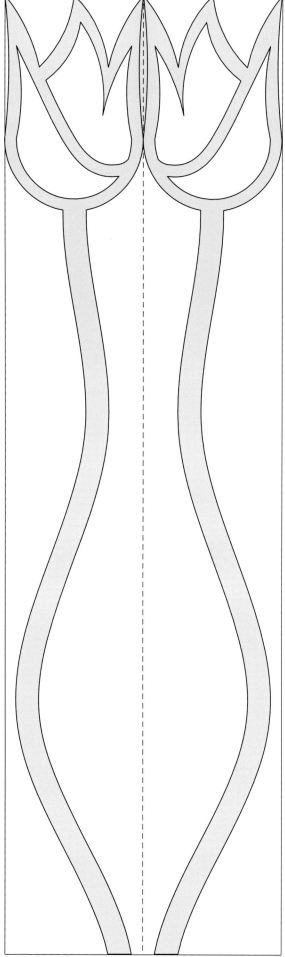

Patterns

Floral Arrangement

Photocopy at 100%

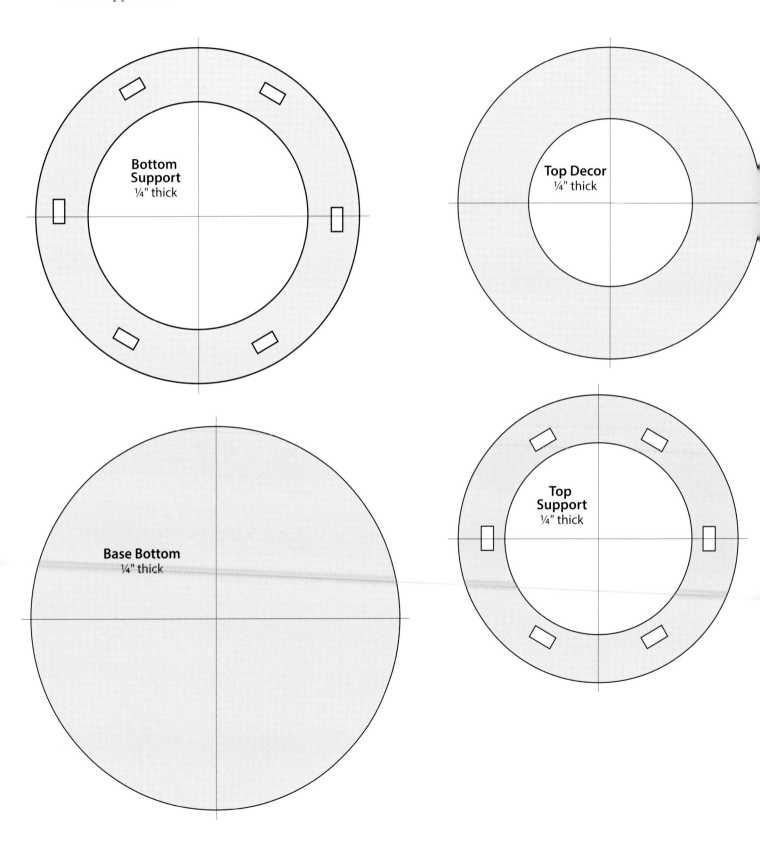

Bottom
Support
¼" thick

Top Decor
¼" thick

Base Bottom
¼" thick

Top
Support
¼" thick

Majestic Lighthouses

Photocopy at 100%

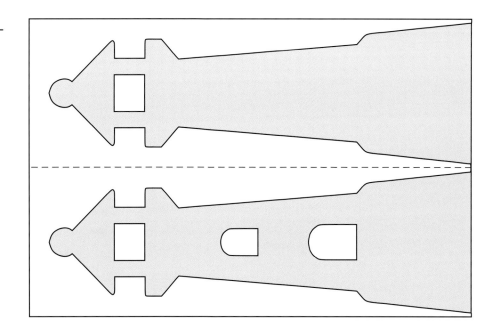

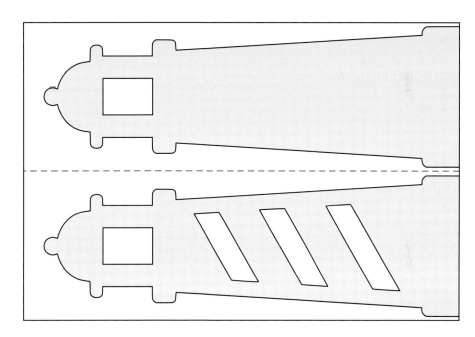

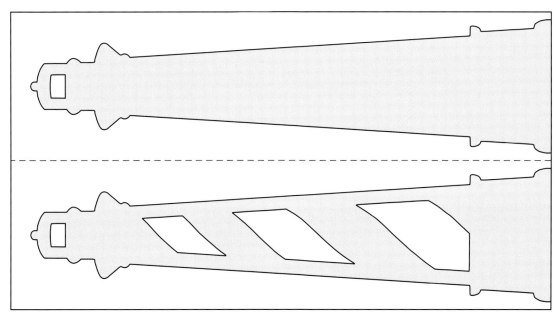

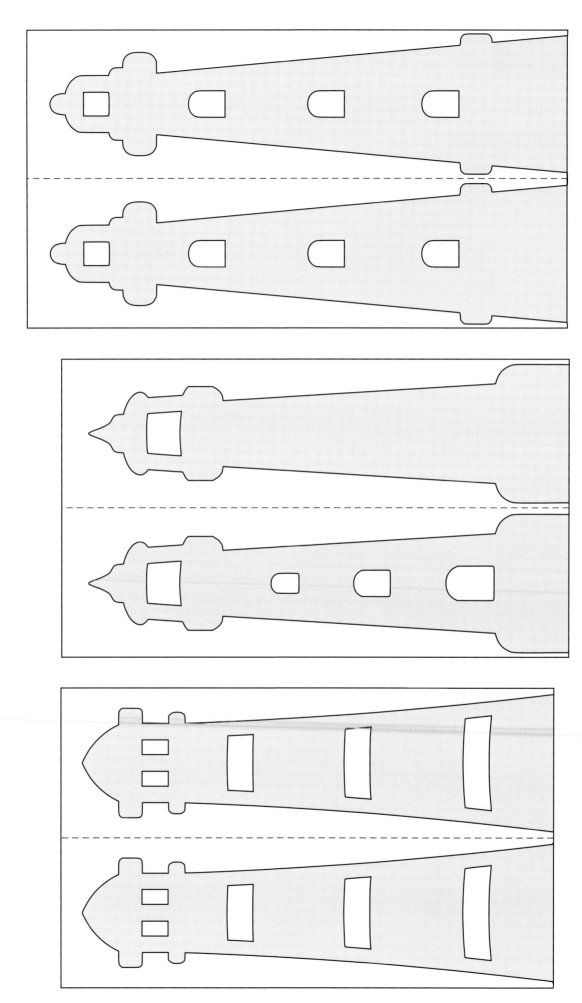

Giraffe Pair

Photocopy at 100%

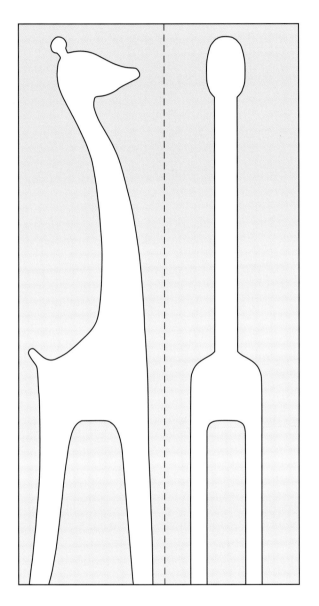
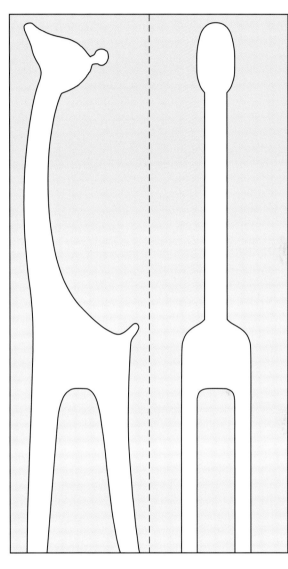

Simple Cacti

Photocopy at 100%

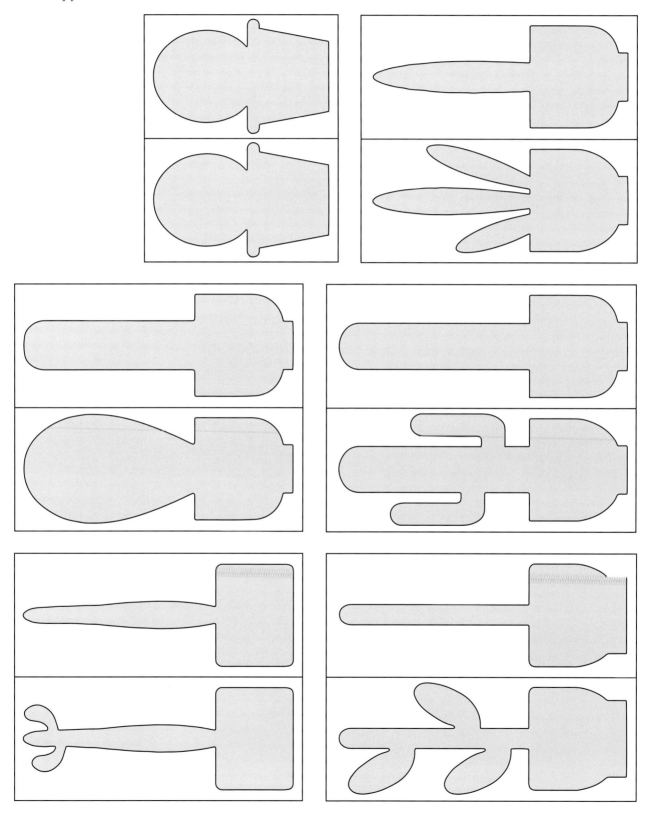

Alighting Butterfly

Photocopy at 100%

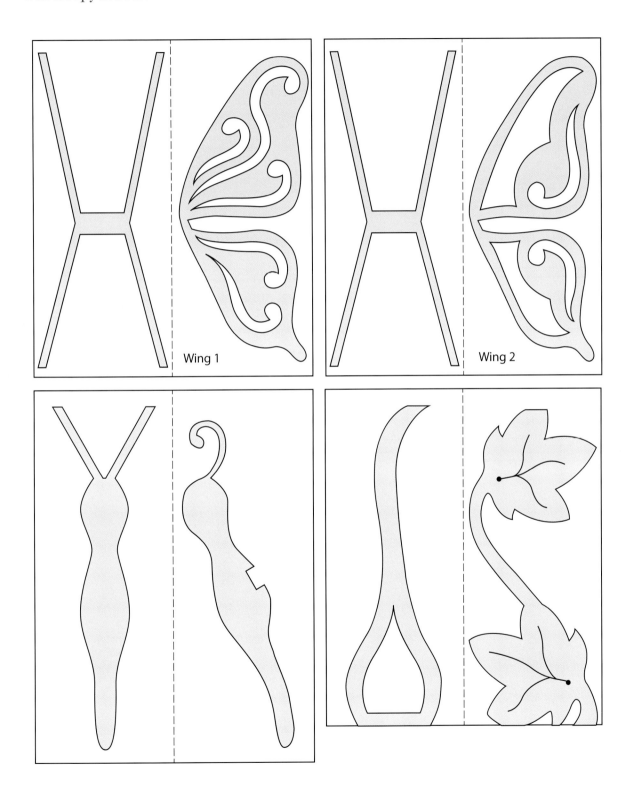

Wing 1

Wing 2

Colony of Mushrooms

Photocopy at 100%

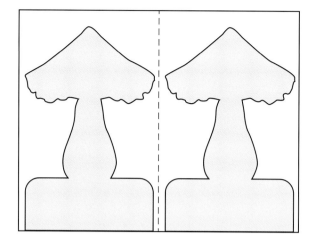

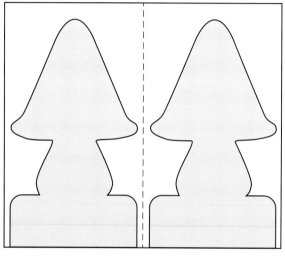

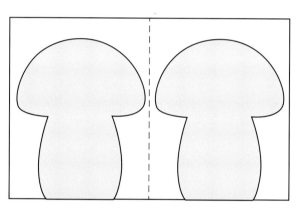

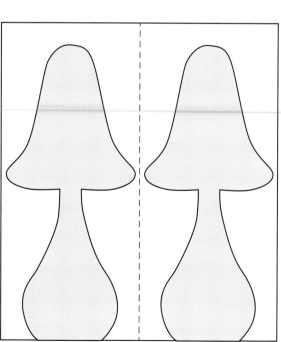

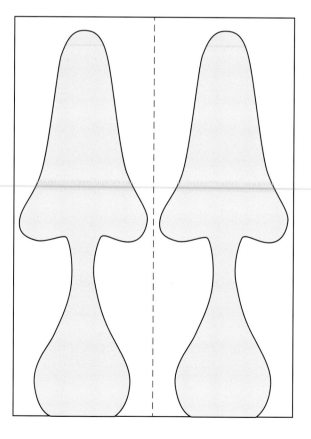

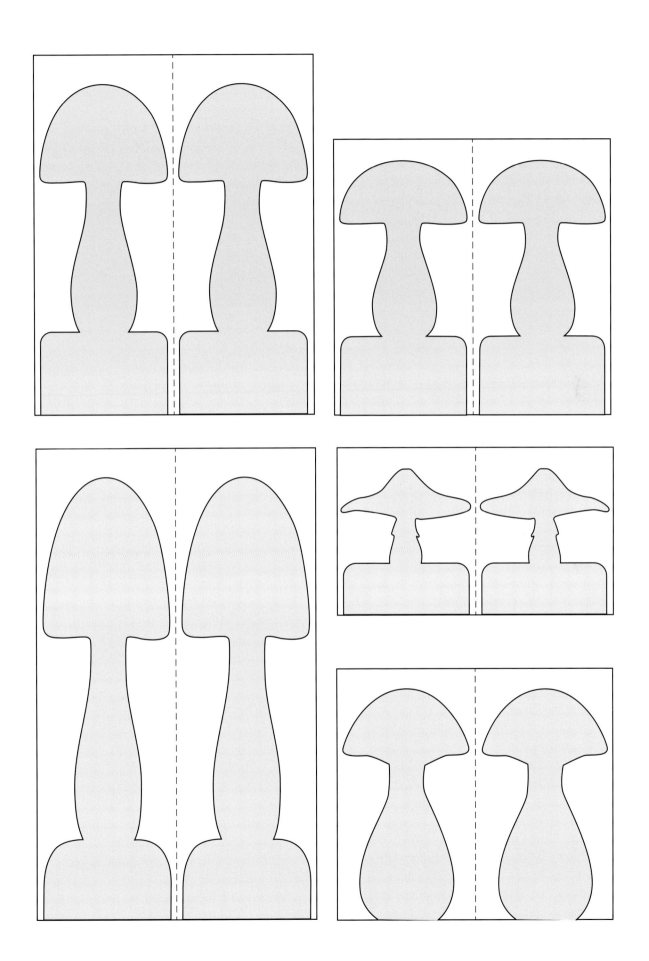

Colony of Mushrooms

Photocopy at 100%

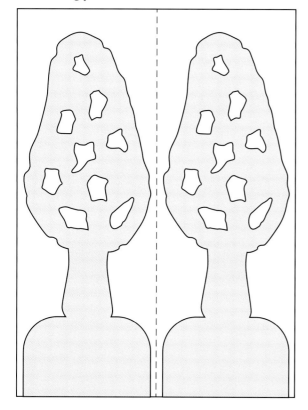

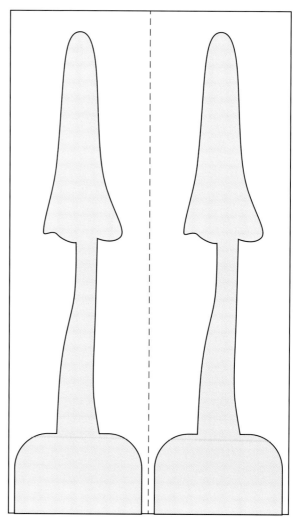

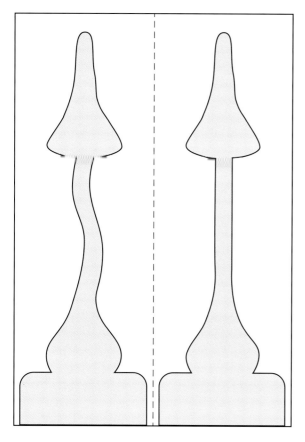

Later, Alligators

Enlarge by 125%

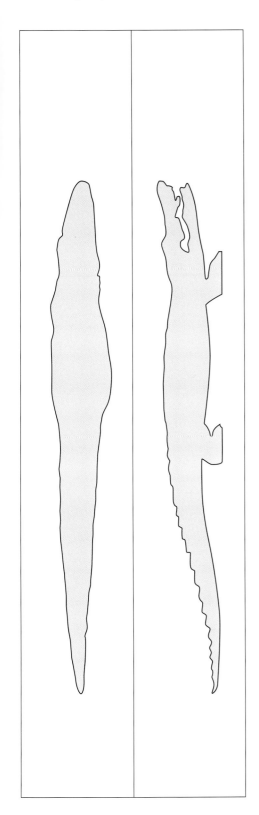
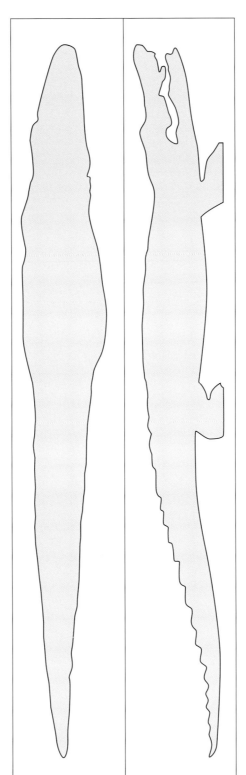
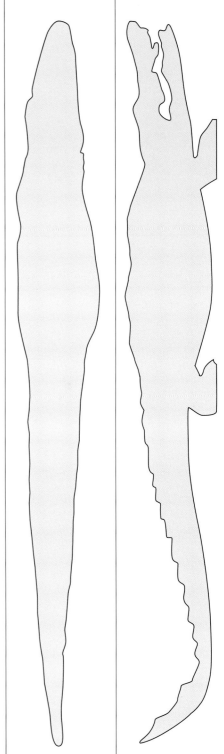

Snake Duo

Photocopy at 100%

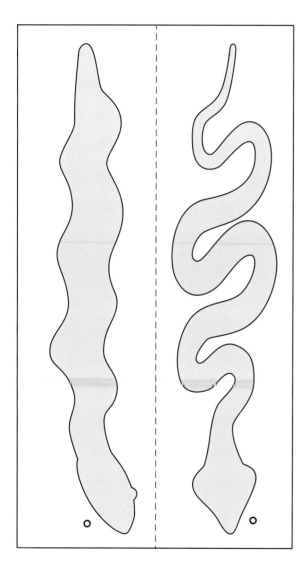

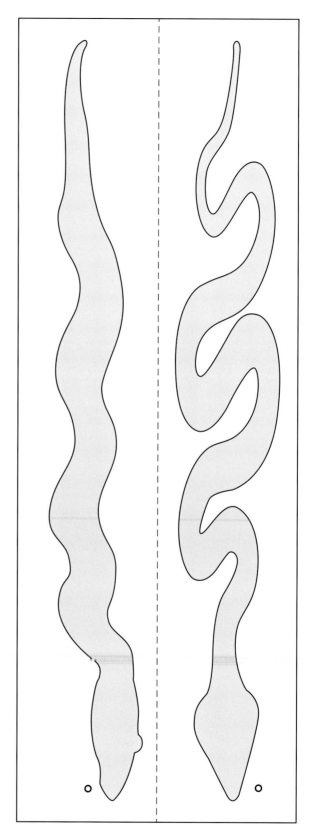

Lampost Light and Jewelry Tree

Enlarge by 110%

Autumn Leaves

Photocopy at 100%

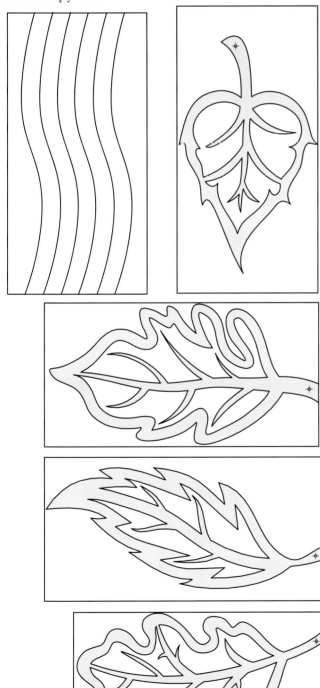

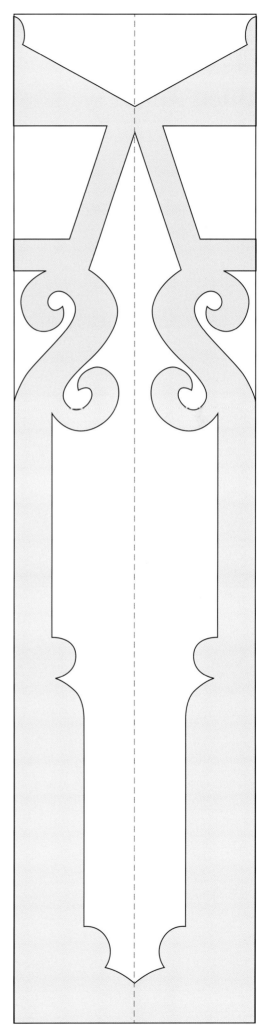

Gilded Angel

Photocopy at 100%

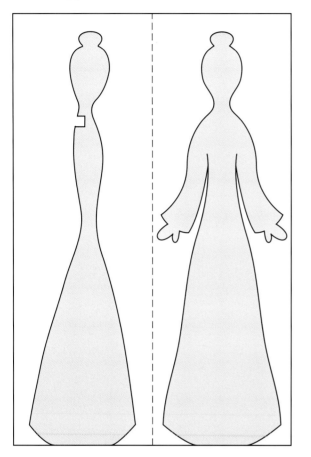

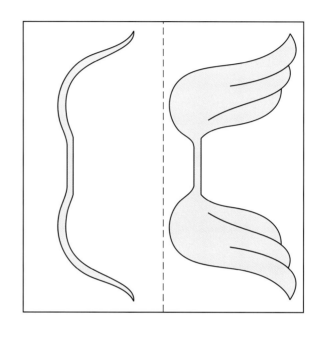

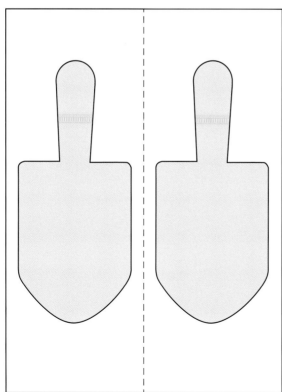

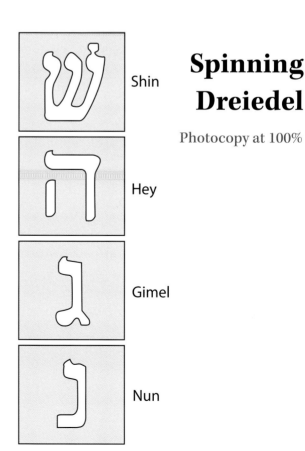

Shin

Hey

Gimel

Nun

Spinning Dreiedel

Photocopy at 100%

Santa's Reindeer & Sleigh

Photocopy at 100%

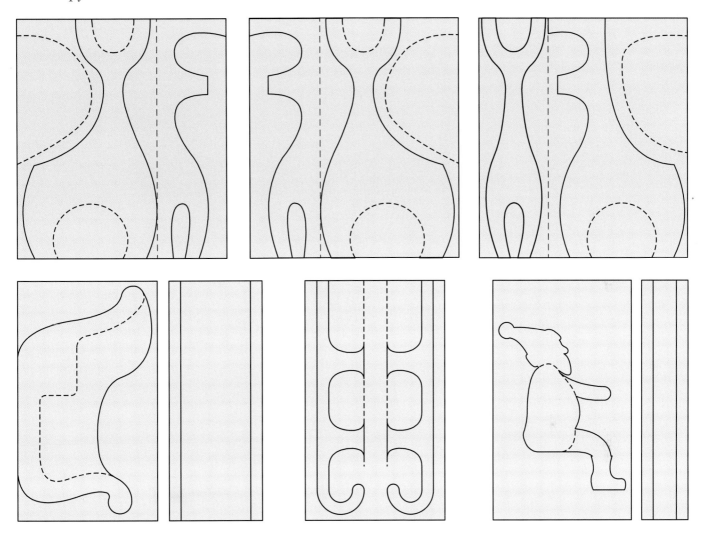

Natural Barrettes

Photocopy at 100%

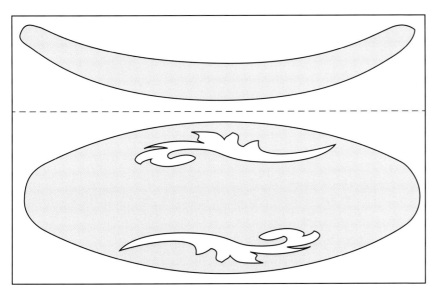

Air Plant Holders

Photocopy at 100%

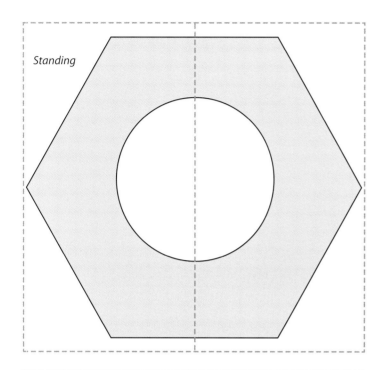

Standing

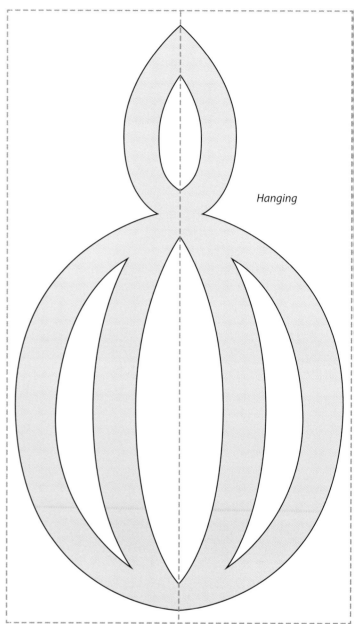

Hanging

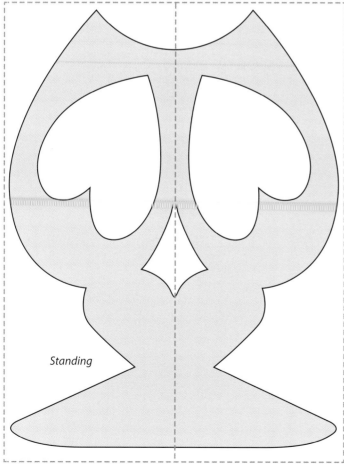

Standing

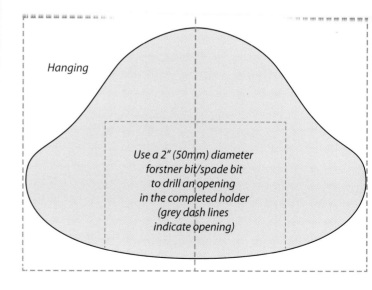

Hanging

Use a 2" (50mm) diameter
forstner bit/spade bit
to drill an opening
in the completed holder
(grey dash lines
indicate opening)

Patterns

Citrus
Glass
Charms

Photocopy at 100%

Air Plant Holders

Photocopy at 100%

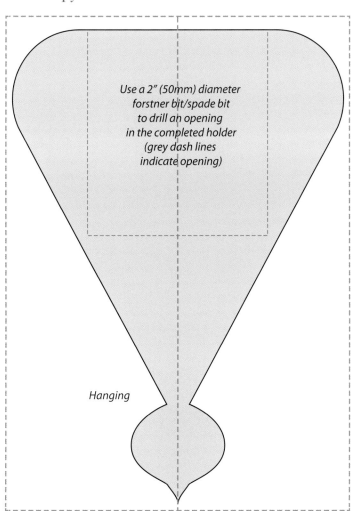

Use a 2" (50mm) diameter forstner bit/spade bit to drill an opening in the completed holder (grey dash lines indicate opening)

Hanging

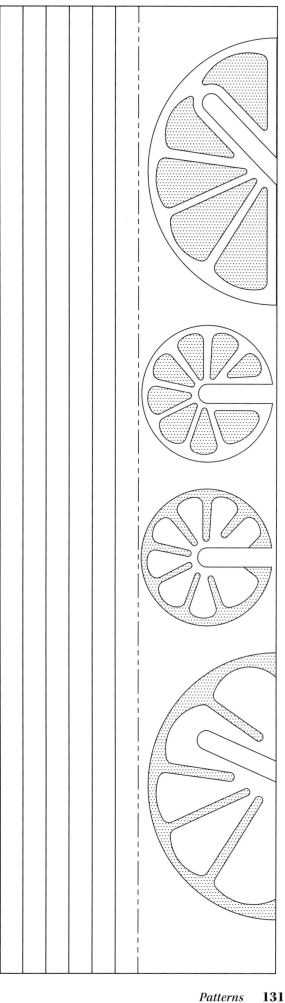

Eiffel Tower Desk Sitter

Photocopy at 100%

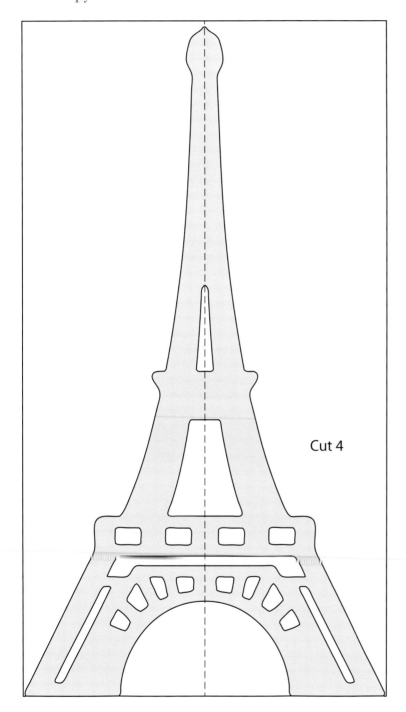

Cut 4

Picnic Lanterns
Photocopy at 100%

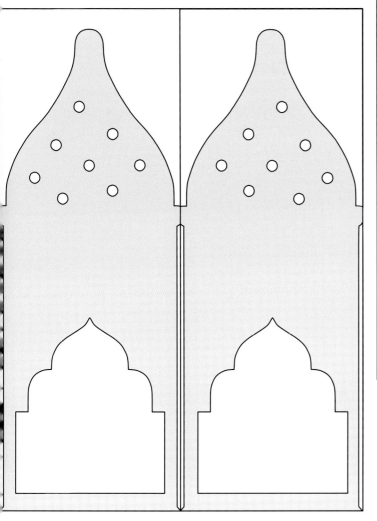

Fretwork Vase
Photocopy at 100%

Opposing Forces Bookends

Photocopy at 100%

Pattern parts within the same outline color should be kept together.

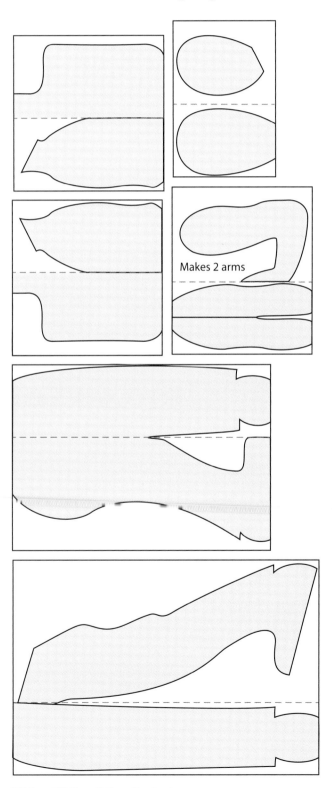

Makes 2 arms

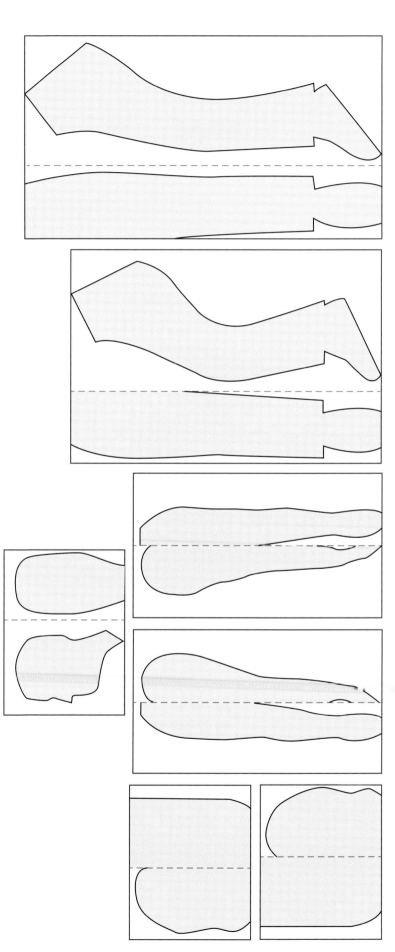

Magnetic Tic-Toc-Toe Game

Photocopy at 100%

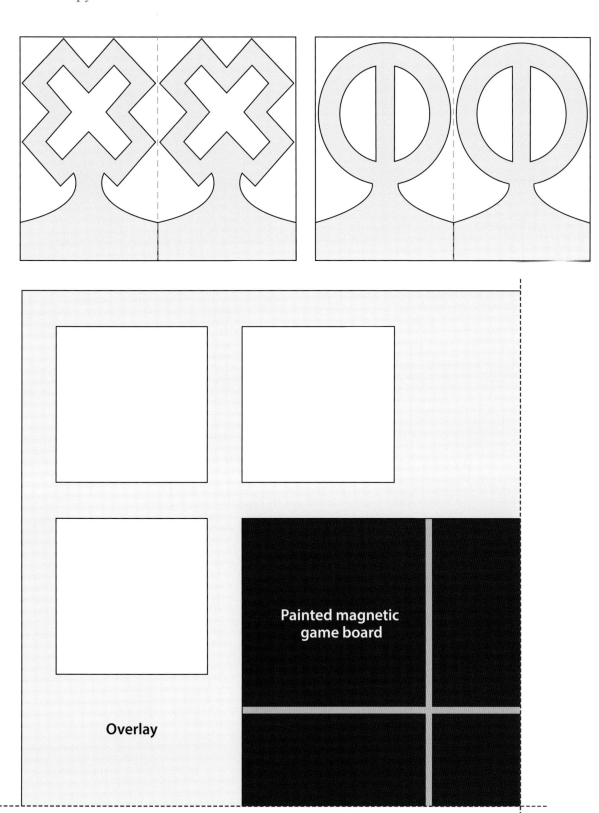

Overlay

Painted magnetic game board

Hardwood Chess Set

Photocopy at 100%

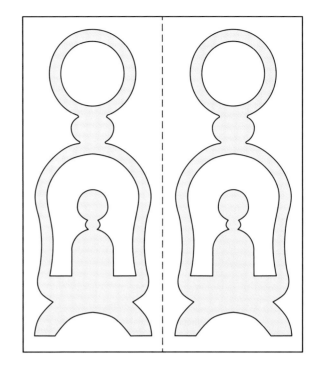

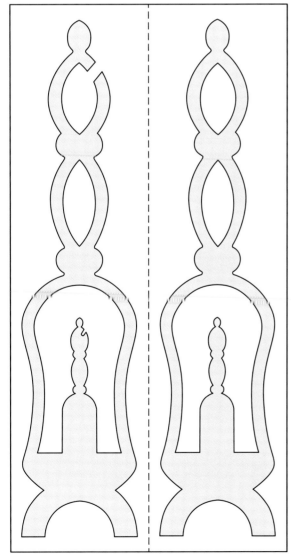

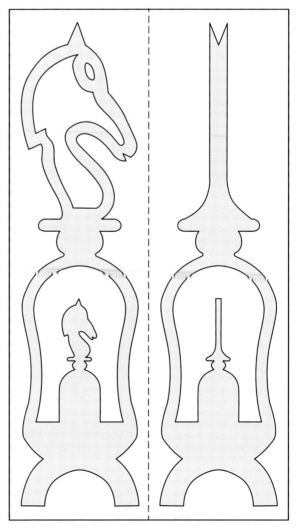

Hardwood Chess Set

Photocopy at 100%

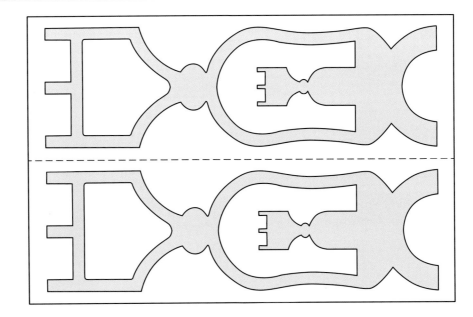

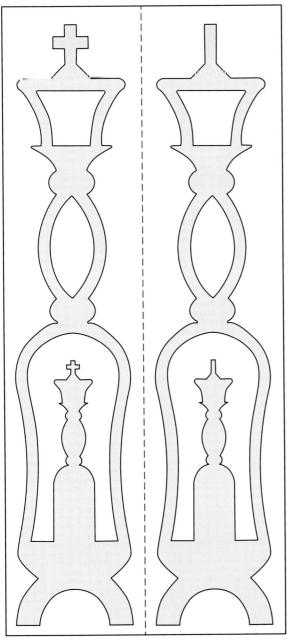

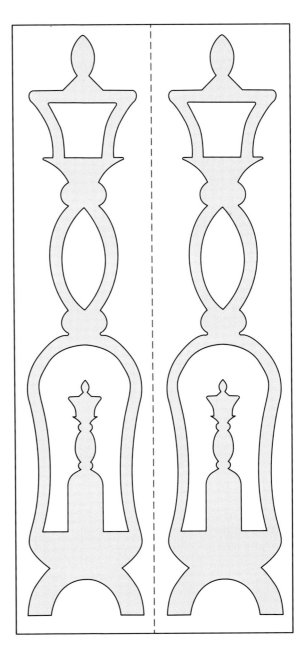

Compound Candle Holders

Photocopy at 100%

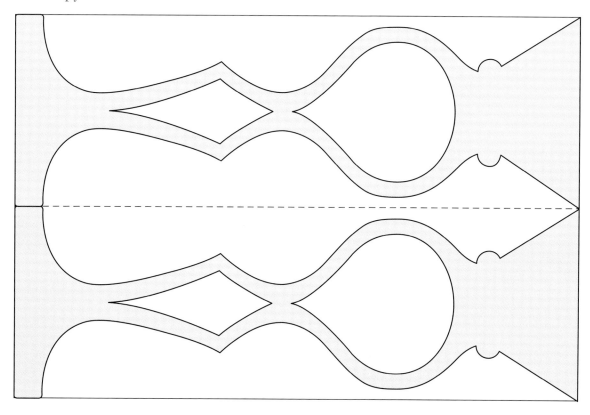

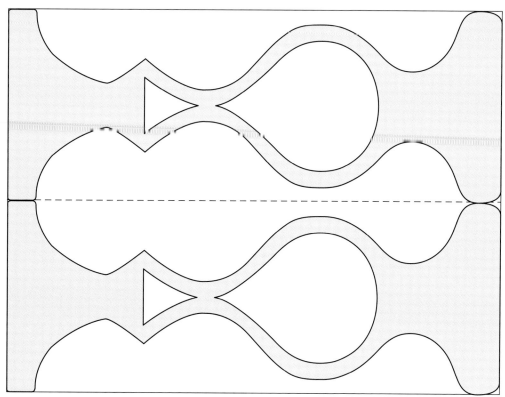

Easy Vase

Photocopy at 100%

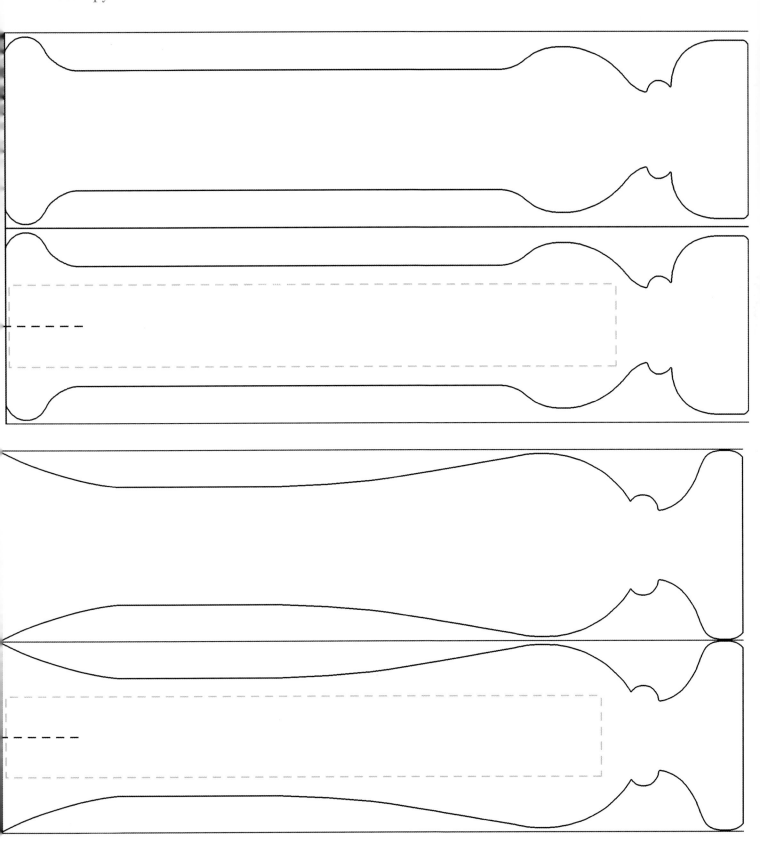

Easy Vase

Photocopy at 100%

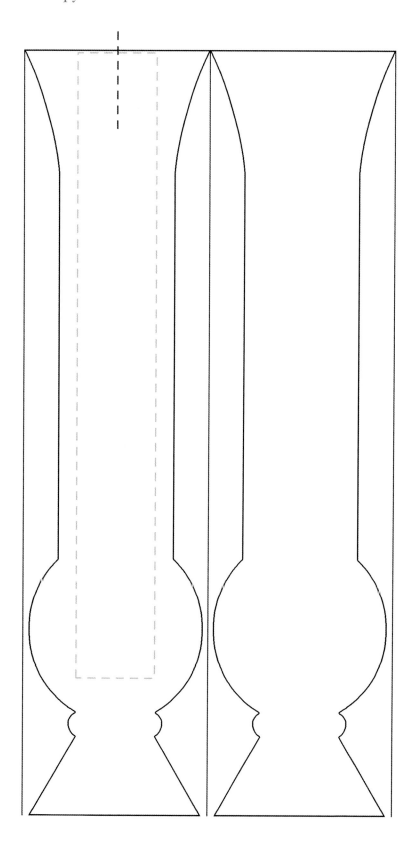

Index

Note: Page numbers in *italics* indicate projects (and patterns). Page numbers in **bold** indicate designer/author bios.

Index

About the Authors

Al Baggetta is a retired English teacher and former musician who took a liking to scroll sawing. Visit his pattern site at baggetta.com.

Dennis Knappen is a scroll saw artist based in Dayton, Tennessee. He and his family have run ArtCrafters, a gallery and art supply business in downtown Dayton, since 2009.

Sue Mey lives in Pretoria, South Africa. To see more of her work, including a wide variety of patterns and pattern-making tutorials available for purchase, visit scrollsawartist.com. She can be contacted at suem@storage.co.za. Her pattern book, *Lighted Scroll Saw Projects*, is available from schifferbooks.com and other outlets.

Ronald Nelson is a scientist from South Africa who lives in Sweden and has been woodworking for just over a year. He makes a number of wooden items, some of which are available at etsy.com/shop/Induku. More of his work is on display at indukudesign.com.

Fred and Julie Byrne live on the Fens in Cambridgeshire, England. They are the authors of *Success with Scrollsaws*, which is available at www.FoxChapelPublishing.com. For more of their work, visit their Website at www.picturesinwood.co.uk.

Charles Mak is a semi-retired businessperson and amateur woodworker in Calgary, Canada. He enjoys writing, authoring shop tips, teaching, and woodworking with both power and hand tools. His e-mail address is: thecanadianwoodworker@gmail.com.

Clayton Meyers has been using a scroll saw since he was 6 years old and got into compound scrolling about 15 years ago. He currently works as a product development engineer in Northern Indiana and is married with two kids. Find more of his work on Etsy at ClaytonsPatterns.

Diana Thompson of Theodore, Alabama, was the author of numerous articles and books about compound cutting. For more of her work, visit foxchapelpublishing.com. Sadly, Diana passed away in 2022, but her legacy and contributions to the scroll sawing community live on.

Jim Kape lives in Chandler, Arizona. Jim's compound chess sets have won numerous awards, including people's choice in *Scroll Saw Woodworking & Crafts'* Best Project Design Contest. Contact Jim on the SSW&C message board at www.scrollsawer.com/forum.

Michelle Martin lives near Atlanta. In addition to scrolling, she enjoys needlework and watching classic movies.

Stephen Miklos designs and builds Carrot Creek Mountain Dulcimers, using his scroll saw to create unique sound holes and decorative inlaid flourishes that set his instruments apart. His scrolling and design work is also expanding, and he works and teaches at the Woodworkers' Club in Norwalk, Connecticut. See his instruments and scroll saw designs at www.carrotcreek.com.

Dave Van Ess is a retired engineer living in Chandler, Arizona. He has been woodworking for 40 years and scrolling for 30. He is the president of Arizona Woodworkers (a greater Phoenix area woodworking club) and volunteers one day a week teaching woodworking to four-year-olds at a local day care.